The Scoop on Ruth

All in the Family, Sense and Nun-sense, Along the Way, The "P" Source

Ruth M. Penksa, gnsh

authorHOUSE®

AuthorHouse™
1663 Liberty Drive
Bloomington, IN 47403
www.authorhouse.com
Phone: 1-800-839-8640

Published by AuthorHouse 10/22/2014

ISBN: 978-1-4389-5360-1 (sc)

ABOUT THIS BOOK
You and Me and God

"The Scoop on Ruth" is a revelation of a life journey told in simple episodes, parables. They are stories with scriptural implications. They are my experiences and they may be yours as you unravel each parable and discover where God is in the rubble- the irregular, broken stones- of our lives.

We live in a time of contemporary parable experiences where trust is offered to science and relationships bow to personal gratification. Unlike the parable where the wild flowers are in a posture of trust allowing God to clothe them with their perfection, in the modern parable, human dignity rests on a perilous Petri dish, stewardship fails to serve the poor and the earth, and life-swapping genetics denies the power of the cross.

Ste. Marguerite d'Youville, founder of the "Grey Nuns", called out in prayer: "Father, the origin of all sanctity, give us the true desire of our perfection."

"Father" has dignified all that I am, all that being is. This is the one who knows my name, who called me from the warmth of a mother's womb into the palm of his hand. The Word was spoken, all was claimed as good, as holy; all is sustained in the hand of his Providence. And, so, all being, all life is destined to its particular perfection, its call to holiness.

When I pray "give us the desire of our perfection: I am in touch with my need to give myself to God so that God may give himself to me.

"The Scoop on Ruth" offers the reader a time to listen to someone's story. Then it invites the reader to a time away from today- a time to remember one's own parables, and the time to discover where God was doing God's thing.

A friend suggested the title after one of my parables- "The chocolate Cover-up". We chatted about possible titles. She doodled as we spoke, then, passed a sketch and its title to me..."The Scoop On Ruth".

DEDICATION

*a Paraphrase from an Anonymous Poem
to Those Who are in My Life or Memory*

To you Mom and Dad and Family all…

> What brought us together you and I
> I think I know the Who and Why
> 'cause parents and family are gifts of love
> And our life bond was planned by the One above

To you my Sisters who've shared this journey…

> What was that call we heard you and I
> I think its sound demanded a reply
> 'cause there were Grey Nuns serving all in need
> And our vows and hands, gift-offerings, bearing God's seed

To you named and unnamed who've lifed my days…

What brought us to share time and space you and I
I think those moments are from God on High
'cause we all need to grow, to become who we are
And you walked with me a while leading me to find my star

Discover
Hidden Treasures

To my God from whom all good things flow…

What makes one pen his thoughts you or I
I think there's a movement a passion to satisfy
'cause there are thoughts deep within each soul
And readers like you paused to hear the words toll

KEN'S PREVIEW

A Sneak Peek

I approached a colleague and friend, himself a writer, with the first pages of my book. Would this book be something that would invite the interest of the general public? What editorial comments might he offer? His opinion and comments would either cut me short or spur me on.

His comments overwhelmed me and encouraged me!

"Sister, humor is your winning mark in writing. You are able to capture the moment and create a scene that I can identify with in so many ways, not one or two but in numerous episodes."

"I absolutely loved reading your book. There was no favorite chapter- all had special meaning and significance. All in the Family was very light hearted with a special treatment of tenderness."

"Sense and Nun-sense is probably my favorite. It is your humility and your down to earthiness that will prevail… I love the symbolism in your writing and would love to see the scenes played before a crowd."

"Sister Ruth, you are a gifted writer and I welcome more and all of your writing previews with scenes which can definitely be used to tell a story (parable) or to just make an audience laugh or cry."

"Thank you for sharing your work. I had nothing to edit except to mention that you do use exclamation points (!!!!) like I do. A standard story should have no more than twenty !!!!!!!!!!!!!!!!!!!!!!. Yes, I'm guilty...too."

Take care and Happy June!
    Ken
p.s. There I go!!!...just can't stop what feels right- agree?

Dr. Ken Barnes
Ass't. Academic Dean
Erie Community College- city
121 Ellicott St. Buffalo NY 14203

ABOUT ME

An Author?

I was born Ruth M. Penksa. Later in life I would become a Grey Nun of the Sacred Heart. But, an author...me?

I am retired from Erie Community College in Buffalo New York. There I served as Campus Minister for 25 years. I was adjunct professor of Spanish and Philosophy of Religion at ECC and of Spanish at d'Youville College.

My work in Campus Ministry opened the door to yearly study conferences in many States throughout the U.S. in the 25 years. In addition, I have had the opportunity, through grants and volunteer experiences, to spend time in Mexico, Peru, Ecuador, and Bolivia.

I was born and grew up in Buffalo New York. When I entered the Grey Nuns, I lived and served in Yardley, Melrose Park, Mahanoy City (Pennsylvania). and in Corona (NY City), Eden and Buffalo New York.

These places, offered me many experiences of teaching including: elementary level, high school Spanish and religion teacher, producer and director of student plays, principal of a Catholic grade school, adult religious education, religion teacher formation and the RCIA...

I enjoy theatre and movies, reading and crossword puzzles. Currently I am a student of Philosophy in a local certificate program.

I love to write! Finally I have found a way- by writing this book based on my life experiences.

The Scoop on Ruth
Contents

PART I
All in the Family- Growing Up Penksa

Part II
Yardley Beckons- Sense & Nun-sense

Part III
Along the Way- Defining Moments

PART IV
A Creative Pen (ksa) – The "P" Source

All in the Family
Growing Up Penksa

Somewhere in a box, an album, a wall or a memory, there are pictures that take us back to family experiences. I think of the familiar 118 Pine Street, a place where we spent many a Sunday...in the days when Sundays were filled with Mass and family visits. And when those days were no more, people walked in and out of our home, our memory ...and our life.

AN APPLE THAT DAY

Memories of the goings on in our home bring both scenes of joy and sadness, remembered experiences of laughter and tears, and yes, the then unspoken wisdom of the woman Sophie.

Sophie, my mother, had presented her husband with four children- a girl, a boy and a set of twins. We grew up in her garden of care, trusting there would always be food on the table, clean clothes to wear, and a warm bed that offered comfort and a sense of security, and always a mother's welcoming heart.

People were always welcome in our home. Late night coffee and chatting took place at our kitchen table. The dining room table turned from the after school homework site into gatherings for games like "garbage" or "monopoly". The small screened living room TV welcomed a Friday evening variety of kids to watch scary movies and eat mom's homemade pizza, fresh from the oven. And there was the front porch where we might fight for a seat on the glider or play a game of chess on the porch railing.

Mom ventured into the work field. I remember her being a parachute inspector, a laundry clerk, and working on line in a swimming pool factory. For enjoyment, mom played in a drum corps, marching in holiday parades or lawn fetes, beating out practiced tunes on her snare drum.

Out of these places of employment and pastime activity came a clear message of the affection folks had for mom and her for them. Often, her associates, alone or with their families, visited announced or unannounced, sharing a bit of mom's hospitality.

That day, we had gathered on the front porch to enjoy a leisurely spring afternoon. One of mom's work mates appeared. He was an unkempt kind of character, poor, whose job was to sweep floors. He wore a long overcoat, perhaps heavier, and longer than the temperature that day called for. Mom greeted him with the same graciousness and hospitality as any guest who dropped by. After a bit, our guest asked if he might go into the house for a glass of water. After his drink of water, he bid us good-bye and hurriedly walked away. I noticed the bulges of his coat

3

pockets. "He took apples from our kitchen" I advised my mom. "He's a thief." But my mom knew the truth. "He's hungry", she said. From our garden of plenty, she allowed him our apples and entrusted us with a gospel lesson.

There was a garden in Eden. There was a woman in the garden story named Eve. And, as the story goes, the woman Eve, God's garden guest, took an apple that day. Her bite into this forbidden fruit caused havoc through the generations of humanity and of nature. Was Eve hungry in the wrong way? Was she starving to be what she could not be- God?

Despite Eve's misguided choice, the Gardener-God, who asked: "Have you been eating of the tree I forbade you to eat?" would offer her forgiveness at his own expense, in "the fullness of time." But, there would be other days and other apple takers. These might have hungers that need to be satisfied if they would survive. They are in our midst and may be wearing long coats, sleeping outside in all elements, looking unkempt...

Perhaps they cry out for a drink of water or a piece of fruit.

The Gardener-God's Son came in "the fullness of time" and he comes with good news for them and for us. He prompts us to recognize Him. "When did we see you hungry"? I think of the guest of a simple housewife, a factory laborer, my mother, welcoming one of these into her home...with an apple… that day.

4

ABBA, ABBA MAC

"Your dad is the funniest person I know!" The words reflected the relationship of Pat and Mack- Pat my dad's best friend. Pat and my Mack were good buddies. Work, music, laughs, spectator sports, beers! These were the guy things that brought them together, only the outward signs of what was a deep friendship. Pat probably knew Mack better than I ever did.

My Abba, my Mack, was a simple man whom I will always remember bent over his work bench. His was not the expected tool bench but, rather a kind of desk topped with all the parts of the watches he was repairing. As long as I can remember Mack had his "bench" where he spent most of his after work hours at his avocation- repairing watches. I wonder what he was thinking as he carefully and quietly treated each watch. His hands worked deliberately and skillfully, much like a surgeon's, invading intimate parts and returning them to good health.

Yes, my Mack was a simple man. This simplicity was marked by a kind of poverty. He owned only one dark suit and one grey suit, always wore a starched white shirt and a tie to work. Mack had no wardrobe to speak of, no sweaters, no sport clothes. He always looked the same. That poverty extended to "things". Mack had no things. He never had a car, never had sports equipment because he was a spectator, never collected anything... It seems that he was surrounded by things that never had his name on them... except for his watch bench.

But, there were the instruments- his guitar, saxophone, violin and piano. I cannot remember when they were no longer there, when Mack plucked the guitar strings for the last time. Each of these saw its day. They were the remnants of Saturday night hoe downs when family members gathered and played and sang for hours into the night- Uncle Louie on the fiddle, Dad with his guitar and Mom with her harmonica sending strains of Red River Valley or You are My Sunshine through a house of sleeping kids. Hoe downs became polkas when the "Penkson Melody Ramblers" of the 1930s- John, Joe, Mack and Tony Penksa, played at weddings and even on the radio. The music faded, quietly, outside of my memory, no date or event to lock their final use in Mack's music history.

We didn't talk much, Mack and I. I often envy Sheila, my friend, who would share a beer with Mack. It was more than a beer. It was a time of story sharing and I missed it because I never drank a beer with Mack.

A bit of secrecy surrounded Mack. There were skeletons in the closet. The wedding picture with the wrong date was quietly removed when I questioned it. Mack never shared the story when the closet revealed that great grandpa was a priest.

What about Mack's spiritual life? That seemed to remain in his personal closet and even beer never coaxed it out. When I look back, I am sorry we never talked, especially about God. I only remember Mack going to Mass and Communion once. It was the Feast of the Holy Family. We stood together at the communion rail, Mack and Mom, my three brothers and I. Mickey, age 9, whispered: "If you don't know what to do, Dad, just watch me."

Something of that secret, or privacy, about Mack and God was discovered after Mack died.

It was revealed in a flat, white wafer called opwatki. The Polish have a New Year's Eve custom of sharing this opwatki, each breaking a piece from the larger one and offering a New Year's greeting. Christmas cards often contained a piece of opwatki assuring one that he is being prayed for. After Mack died, mom was tidying up the bedroom. When she lifted the mattress of his bed her eyes fell on a small, white piece of opwatki-opwatki tucked between mattress and bed spring. How did it get there? Why was it there?

For me, that broken wafer, that hidden piece of opwatki, said out loud what I never heard Mack speak. I think it was Mack's truth, his faith, tucked away in the intimacy of his heart and in that secluded space between mattress and bed spring. Mack's faith, safe in these private places! Now, in death, his faith was finally exposed. He must have believed in the words of Jesus, "This is my body given up for you." I think he believed it so much that he saw in that unconsecrated wafer what he wanted in this time of his physical suffering- to be close to Jesus.

Abba, Abba Mack I am sorry that I never drank a beer with you.

Jesus knew who his father was, his Abba. He called him by that name which matches our "daddy" or "pop". But, how do I relate to God? How do I approach the invisible mystery that is God, who is my Father in heaven, the one to whom I pray in secret? I pray what I have learned by sharing the story Jesus tells, "Our Father in heaven...Give us this day our daily bread..." I listen to Jesus, the Son, whose stories assure me that, "when you have seen me you have seen the Father." Jesus urges me on. He invites me to recognize him in the breaking of the bread. He continues, "Take and drink"...and the rich story continues to break open, to reveal the reality, the truth, of the one who is hidden in the simplicity of bread and wine. I am invited to the table, to choose to share in this story, to know the one whose secret is revealed when I eat and drink.

Abba, Abba Father... I delight in you through that consecrated "opwatki" and the wine I drink offered by your Son. But, how many Macks have clung, alone, to a semblance of their Abba...hungry, and have we forgotten to invite- "watch me"!

THE RUN AWAY

A stark, bright ray of light awakened me from dreamless sleep as I lay huddled on a park bench. I moved throwing off my only cover, the fetal-body warmth that had warded off the damp night air. Then a voice belonging to the figure that gradually took shape as my eyes accepted the light and my surroundings. It was a cop! "What are you doing here?"

When you are thirteen years old and running away from home, all you need is a policeman to interrupt your journey! After a brief interrogation, I was returned, bike and run-away bundle, to an anxious mom.

Quo vadis? Where was I going? After a typical mom-kid argument, I had packed a few necessities and took off on my recent acquisition, a thirteen dollar bike. Destination- Aunt Frances' home where I was sure to be comforted in my tribulation and assured that I was a mistreated and misunderstood child. And, definitely, I had made the right decision to run away.

Aunt Frances, my mom's sister, was also my God-mother. She lived about fifteen miles from us. I had made the trip by bike frequently under better circumstances. Often I made the trip there after school and returned after breakfast the next morning in time for school. I think it may have taken about two hours each way.

On this occasion, however, I started out but was greeted by an unexpected weather condition- strong wind. I had pedaled against its strength for several minutes when I realized that today was not a good afternoon for this particular escape to Aunt Frances'. Since my trek had ended very near the park, also just a few minutes from home, I went there and took refuge on a park bench to ponder my situation and re-strategize. In the midst of my planning I had found respite on the uncomfortable bench. Evening and sleep fell upon the unaware run away. It was here that I was discovered and the direction I was headed now led to home.

When I think back of childhood days and mom-daughter relationships, what strikes me is the unconditional love of a parent for a child. How does a mom or a dad, continue to love an unruly off-spring? To forgive before a penitential word is spoken?

Day to day peer relationships aren't like that. On the job relationships aren't based on that kind of love. Even sibling ties come unloosed under stressful situations. The world community fails daily as it measures relationships by getting even.

But, there is the mom who welcomes home her prodigal daughter. Her loving response echoes the parable: "We are going to have a feast, a celebration."

I wonder why the younger son in Luke's parable really took off. What lured him away from the comfort of a parent who obviously loved him so deeply? How far can a daughter or a son run away from home and love? A more illusive question for me is "how could the father be so welcoming, hold the child in his heart as though nothing had ever changed his love for the one called prodigal?"

My mom and yours are called the first teachers. They are the imitation of the God whose language of love is burned into their hearts, whose flames are indistinguishable. Like the father in the parable, my mom always gifted me when there was a hint of separation in our relationship. No "so you're back, huh!" Rather, I was wrapped in her warm embrace. She would quickly go the store and return with a gift for me, a blouse or sweater. Did I need a cup of hot chocolate? The welcome, the gift, the drink- all symbols of a deep and abiding, unconditional, celebrated love.

Perhaps Jesus told this parable not so much to remind us of the Father-God and the love he has for us but to let us know that we can experience that love between one another. It may be the key to the commandment that we honor our father and mother because they are the living truth of the existence of unconditional love.

THE GIRL FROM KOSCIUSKO STREET

East side Buffalo! Kosciusko and its parallel streets stretched out to Broadway, to the Rivoli Show, to the Broadway Market and the famous "998". This was a little Poland. Third generation, second and even first generation Catholic Poles greeted each other: "Niech bedie pochwalony Jesus Chrystus", praised be to Jesus Christ.

Kosciusko Street was Patsy's venue. My cousin grew up there in the culture of her parents and neighbors, of her Church and school, of playmates who spoke the languages of their two worlds. Today, 998 is no more, the Rivoli is gone and finally, Patsy's house is no more. But a ride through the area and a stop at the Broadway Market enliven the remnant images of the once bustling little Poland.

Kosciusko Street was a double transfer, bus and streetcar trip, from my home in the northwest corner of the City along the Niagara River. It was a trip I made often. It was a trip made by an only girl in the family in search of an "adopted" sibling playmate. Thus Patsy from the East Side and Ruthy from the Northwest enjoyed the experience of being more than cousins, "sister-playmates".

Now, as often happened, Patsy would be at our house after a family visit and then stay overnight. But one day together seemed so little. "Stay another day," I'd plead. The positive response only had one condition: "...if you go to my house and get me some play clothes." No problem. I always accepted the condition and crossed town, day or evening, using the double transfer method and returned with the desired wardrobe.

And just what did these sister-playmates do for fun? One favorite was "the Night Club", featuring future singer Patsy S. This required the transformation of the set from kitchen to a dimly lit club scene and for the actors a quick wardrobe adjustment.

Lights off! Glasses with the drink of the day (mostly water or juice) were served to the one guest. The wall lamp spotlighted the attraction of the day. Beautiful strains with words from the latest movie musicals came from the dancing diva. She flitted across the floor of the kitchen-club while the guest raised a glass to toast the performance followed by claps of approval.

Such was our imaginative world. It was a world not dominated by television but by the creativity inspired by then unrated "G" movies and the freedom to play. Here a child might express her thoughts of one day becoming a performer, a singer and dancer.

How does this child-world finally grow into adulthood? No, Patsy did not become a club performer. That fantasy is realized in her love of music and those singers who inspired her in the 50s. Her performance over the years has been an expression that emerges from her original roots as a girl from Kosciusko Street.

Little Poland introduced Patsy to a second language, one that would offer her opportunities to bond with first generation relatives. It would strengthen her to accept its traditions: fidelity in marriage and in religious faith, cleanliness (of the sweep the street variety) and a love of home and favorite polish recipes (of the homemade sausage and potato pancake ilk), to partner with someone to perform a polish polka. All these, Patsy performed like a professional. Yet, her outstanding performance is one that flows from the spirit of a Pearl in her life, from the mother to the daughter... a beautiful spirit of hospitality. Like her Pearl, Patsy welcomes. Her door is open, her laughter inviting, her love and concern shown in her availability and presence to all who sit at her table, who share her placzak.

As one enters into this life-giving performance, one can only respond: "na wieki wieki, Amen"... forever and ever, Amen. We applaud you Patsy!

When we reflect on Jesus' growing up years, we become aware of his performance- as "the son of a carpenter from Nazareth" as a Jewish boy. The boy, son of Jewish parents, Jewish playmates, neighbors speaking Jewish and Arabic, praying in the Synagogue, sharing the Jewish paschal meal...!

As an adult, Jesus gave an outstanding performance of hospitality, one that grew out of his identity as a Jew and flowed from the cherished "pearl" he speaks of in the parable. Hospitality! Didn't he stretch out his arms to open the gates of Heaven, to welcome all? Didn't he care and love so as to forgive sin and heal the sick? Didn't he prepare a meal and invite all to his table?

For all who enter into His life-giving performance, we can only respond: "Forever and ever. Amen".

LITTLE BOY LOST

"Oh no, he's a boy," the proud nine year old corrected. The warm brown curls that framed the almost two year old's face might fool the stranger. But I knew this was my baby brother and I loved him very much.

When mom brought home my new baby brother, already nicknamed in the hospital, the one named Daniel was soon lost and the more affectionate "Sonny" entered my life. My teacher and classmates were informed of this wonderful event by an overjoyed sister. After all, I had been an only child for my first seven years with dolls as my only sibling experience.

Things were different now. I spilled my affection on my new brother. And, as he grew and his hair fell into soft locks, I still knew he was my baby brother. Yet, as was wont to happen, one day the locks fell. It was at Uncle Louie's that mom decided it was time for Sonny's first haircut. I had accompanied my cousins to the movies that day and when we returned I met this brother with skepticism. "No, this can't be my brother." Something of the sibling and the shared years seemed lost when those locks were clipped away.

But the loss was short lived and a growing family would serve to nurture our sibling relationship. Twins entered the family picture. Mom now had three children under two years old. I became a bit of a surrogate. While she tended the needs of two, Sonny and I became inseparable companions. A deep bond developed. Everywhere I was, Sonny was. Mom bathed the twins, then, Sonny and I were tub mates. Mom pushed the wide buggy and I, Sonny in his stroller.

As the three boys grew, household space seemed too small. At the same time, Sonny began to have nightmares. To accommodate these, Sonny and I shared a bed. After one of his nightmares, mom would settle him back in bed assuring him I was there and all would be safe. He felt safe and would rest knowing his sister was nearby.

At times, the deep sibling bond would be demanding. My weekend visit to my God-mother's house- interrupted when Dad came to pick me up. "Your brother has a fever, won't take his bottle, wants you." I loved my brother. I would return and he would recover. Then there was the sneak tactic. I wanted to go home with visiting relatives so that I might spend a weekend with my cousin. At least a half hour before their departure, I would kind of...fade away...and sneak into their car to await the trip to their home. Sometimes it worked and at others, well there went a weekend away. You wonder why my parents gave in. I suppose it was the tears and screaming or the chance of his becoming ill. It was okay, I loved my brother.

It was I who walked Sonny to school on his adventure toward Pre-K. It was a struggle. Somehow our bond was loosening. He would pull away from my hand-hold and race home. It might take a try or two but finally we arrived. Now the bond took hold again and it was he who grasped tightly at my hand, not wanting me to leave.

The bond seemed to loosen more as Sonny grew and school and neighborhood provided him friends and activities for a guy his age. Before long it would be girls and sports and cars. I was losing the "little boy". His interests, his life, the Marine Corps, and love and marriage- all were moving the little boy toward a different path.

For a while, in his first home with his wife, and two children asleep, we shared something of the little boy and sister relationship. We'd gather, Sonny and wife, a friend and I, around their table and talk and talk and talk- burning and sharing the midnight oil. How wonderfully refreshing! Re-nurturing!

I think the "little boy" really drifted away when he chose to move his family to Arizona. Although the stay there was brief, the return did not bring back the old bond. Moments yes, but in time the deep bond went along unnoticed.

———————

Mary and Joseph had a deep bond with the child Jesus. Mary accepted him as gift of God, to mother him. Joseph was willing to take on the role of a nurturing father. Together they offered him a religious home, parental discipline, the tools of a trade. We can picture the beautiful life they shared. Yet, we see the moment when Jesus bends the bond of family, when he, a pre-teen, goes off to do his thing- his "Father's affairs", he says.

Then, at thirty, he drops his trade responsibility and goes off again- to find himself. The babe, the little boy is lost, and a new man emerges. His relationship with family changes. How does Mary feel about her "lost boy"? Things have changed in her household, in her life. A different bond is offered her when, finally from a cross, her once little boy presents her to us: "Woman, behold your son, son behold your mother." Do you wonder how Mary felt at that moment?

We all have or will experience a change in bonded relationships. It is the cost of change and growth and living the life God draws us toward. Must old bonds be severed or loosened? Is there only a season of beautiful bonding that must give way to a new season? What is the feeling of the one for whom the little boy is lost and of the little boy himself?

"I NEVER CLEAN MY GLASSES"

"Glasses, just for reading!" That was the doctor's prescription after a brief examination. I had presented myself because of a case of red, itchy eyes that persisted beyond a reasonable time. What was reasonable for a college freshman? After all, this new student lifestyle demanded many hours of reading. There was the whole array of humanities' courses each with its particular reading list. One might not then be so surprised at eye strain and the need for glasses.

For me wearing glasses was a first. If I was disgruntled at the beginning, I soon realized that wearing them was okay. They relieved the strain brought on by the volumes of required reading and they did not interfere with my other life. Glasses could be put aside when I pitched softball or played third base; they were not necessary for bowling or skiing; I could guard and shoot baskets without them. There was no need for glasses when coaching C.Y.O. teens in competitive sports and directing them in plays.

So in a normal day, glasses were not a burden. After wearing them to do any reading at home, I would slip them off, place them on a lamp table and head for a night's rest. In the morning, the ritual was reversed when I took the glasses and headed off for another college day.

On one particular day, as my class cronies sat in the coffee room during a break time, one of my glass-wearing friends asked me for a tissue so that she could clean her glasses. "Clean your glasses?" I was a bit surprised at that and as I handed her the requested tissue let her know: "I never clean my glasses." Almost in chorus all chimed: "Everyone has to clean her glasses." I denied that action to their unanimous disbelief.

That evening as I chatted with my mom about my day, I told her about the coffee room discussion about cleaning glasses. Her motherly response revealed what I had failed to see: "Of course you never clean your glasses because when you leave them on the lamp table at night I pick them up, clean them and then return them."

There it was, a simple truth, a mom's gift. My mom cleaned my glasses every night. I never saw that, just as I am sure, as I look back, that there

16

were other mom things that I missed over our many years together. Maybe I didn't see them because I wasn't wearing my glasses!

I think about my mom, about mothers, and how they move about quietly taking care of their children's needs- even their adult children. It is easy to see the big things they do. Yet we miss so much, the many small kindnesses they do when we are not looking.

Life is filled with people who touch our lives with their quiet actions. Wearing glasses will not help us to recognize the unspoken kindnesses. Sometimes, we chalk them up to luck or chance or even to a "Thank God" and actually miss that there is a person behind the acts.

We are not alone as we journey through our days, our experiences, our life. God has gifted us along the way with people. They are there to be his hands to guide us, to prompt us, to care for us. If we but look! There was a son who lamented, "What have you given me?", when his father celebrated the return of a prodigal son. What was the father's response? "You are always with me and everything I have is yours."

It is good for us to be mindful of the ones around us and how they are the ones who "clean our glasses."

THE ONE MILE WALK

As I drove past the old homestead on 89 Clay Street I was reminded of Aunt Caroline and her frequent one mile walks to visit my mom. Those visits were interesting because they never lasted long enough to take off her coat but just a pause long enough to enjoy a cup of coffee in the kitchen where coffee was always brewing. One mile for a five minute visit!

I still picture Caroline's visits. Her entry was accompanied with that familiar, "Oh Hellooo". Often what followed was a whispered: "I was just at the Mass of the 'Secret' Heart". I caught the mistake but my chuckle was smothered by my mom's eye of disapproval. Mom was an understanding in-law.

Aunt Caroline was clean but carelessly dressed, slip showing beneath her dress, a hat tipped on her head, purse in hand. But underneath this exterior disguise there was a simple woman, kind, and I suspect one who never had a bad word to say about anyone.

I don't remember grandpa living in the family home on Clay St. But I do remember Caroline and John. But I cannot picture their evenings just sitting around and sharing conversation about their day.

Their two daughters were the rich gift of that union. Other gifts were not as obvious. The younger, was my playmate as I first grew up in the upper area of the family home and then in the house next door. Kids, we were not aware of our parents' lives. Our awareness of life was centered in a world dominated by play and then by our first experiences of school.

The one mile to our new home became a still longer distance in the familiarity of the family we left behind at 89 Clay. Only one visit to that home comes to mind, a wedding party. But brothers stayed close. Uncle John and my dad enjoyed the bond of being brothers and fellow musicians. The girls often visited us on a Sunday and so we experienced their growth into teens and adults and then married women.

But, it was those unusual pop in visits by Aunt Caroline that I picture most vividly. When or where in the midst of my growing up did the "Oh

Hellooos" cease? When did Caroline walk her last mile to our home? When did Caroline begin another walk, a walk into another time and place, a walk into a lover's embrace?

We all take walks. Our "one mile" leads us to different places for different reasons.

I wonder how long Jesus' walk bearing the cross was. When I pray the Stations of the Cross, I pause along his way to think of what was happening along that "mile". I see him wearing the hat of thorns and a garment carelessly covering him. On his shoulders that cross gripped by hands that just a day before passed bread and wine to his friends.

And just where was Jesus going? What would be the end of that walk? Hadn't he said earlier, "I am going to prepare a place for you..."? Now he went to the place of final preparation, Calvary. There people mocked him for his claim now rewarded by nails, and his thirst with vinegar. One of those lifted on a cross near him stilled the mockery with words of faith.

Just what do I make of his walk to that place on Calvary? As we look back, what about the Aunt Carolines who walk into our space? Jesus was able to look upon his neighbor, the thief sharing the ignominy of the moment and change that visit into an eternal welcome.

Those fourteen stations may be a call to us to be mindful of our life walk, a walk into our lover's embrace, and the walk of others into our space and our welcoming embrace.

ALL I WANT FOR CHRISTMAS...

It was Christmas in July celebrated in Riverside Park. The words of the song were flowing from my eight year old brother, through the empty space where new teeth waited to emerge.

"All I want for Christmas is my two front teeth, my two front teeth... All I want for Christmas is my two front teeth, my two front teeth"... he sang over and over. Finally, a prompt from big sister released him from that single line. And in the end, he did win a prize and his accomplishment was noted in the local Review.

Teeth! Mickey finally had his Christmas wish- two new front teeth. They were beautiful teeth and he was proud of them. Of the four children in our family, his were the best. He proudly cared for them. But tragedy struck! It was while on a vacation in Canada, while playing horseshoes. He bent to pick up a horseshoe and somehow his tooth and the stake met with unfriendly results. "My tooth!" he cried out, "my beautiful tooth!" Now the line of a Christmas lyric came to mind as he picked up a beautiful tooth from the ground.

His concern and his care were traits that he extended beyond his "beautiful teeth" to anything he possessed. His bicycle had a special place in our dining room. It was the only one that was immaculately cleaned daily and earned the security of the dining room at night. When he became a driver, his car received a daily wash. Of course the car remained outside but the eye of the owner was upon it.

Every car he owned would become the privileged receiver of Mickey's care. Yet, not all care can stay the harshness of nature. A neighbor's call one morning alerted him to the tree that had fallen during a storm. Yes, Mickey's first car was now crowned by that fallen tree. The lamenting words followed: "My beautiful car".

When he married, he brought his gifts to his family. He surrounded his wife and three boys with the same care that were evident in his care of things. They were the best and he provided the best for them- love, appreciation, response to their needs! He was proud of each son! But the haunting losses of his youth emerged in a most devastating way and fell upon his twenty two year old son.

A parked car! Motor running! Something amiss with the engine! A young man asleep in the back seat! Oven burning heat! Firemen! Burns over all his body head to toe! Perhaps the cry now was both of pain and gratitude: "My beautiful son!" But pain would be the echo of those words when ten years later they were spoken over his son's grave.

The simple Christmas "want" of an eight year old had been sung innocently on a July day. Wants- teeth and cars- received, broken, replaced! Yet, there was the gift of a son. For Mickey the words, "All I want for Christmas…" now linger unanswered.

———————————

There was no Christmas when the young girl Mary was approached by an angel. We do know that there was an expectation of a Messiah. Perhaps in that angelic visit one might sense the strains of that "want". There was a simple song of acceptance- "be it done to me". Mary sang and somehow its strains were repeated in the mystery of the Jews' expectations. Mary becomes the one to bring forth what they wanted.

Angels sang, shepherds watched, and Magi left gifts for the Christmas Gift Himself and perhaps Mary lulled the Child, her beautiful Gift, her Son.

What happened to that beautiful Gift? The prophet Isaiah reveals a description that marks Him a suffering Gift: no stately bearing, spurned, held in no esteem, pierced, harshly treated. Was Mary aware that her Gift, the Messiah, would endure all that and even death on a cross when she first responded to the angel?

The innocent utterance of the young Mary years ago gave the world a Gift, a Son. Mary could not change this now moment of death. For Mary, her "be it done to me", would be her lingering acceptance.

THEY CALL HIM "BIG TOM"

"What's in a name?" a poet once questioned. On a December day near Christmas, my mom gave birth to twins- Thomas and Michael, soon dubbed Tommy and Mickey. No need to identify either as big or little although the firstborn was the bigger twin. And, he remained the bigger of the two in his growing up years as well.

The tag "big" became a marker when another Tom arrived on the block. "Big" and "Little" accurately distinguished the boys by size. Thus, they were christened, as it were, with the tags until...well, my brother is still referred to as "Big Tom" even as he celebrates his adult birthdays. The years have passed and the childhood playmate Toms have grown in adulthood and have gone their separate ways. But the name remains with the descriptive tag..."Big".

At home, Big Tom always prided himself that he was the taller and stronger of the twin siblings. His brother was scrappy and willing to engage in a fight with Big Tom but we often laughed at what was really inevitable, who the champ would be in those kid disputes.

Big Tom was very conscious of his size and body. Even at nine years old he would point to his chest and tell mom that one side was larger than the other. I think it was easy to dismiss that claim with a diagnosis of "pigeon breast" When he participated in a summer swimming class and came home with a cut on the temple he claimed "a fat guy fell on me while running on the tile edge of the pool". Once again a dismissal and a bandage and life went on".

As he grew into a tall lanky teen, Tom loved Elvis and loved that people said he looked just like his music idol. Was that why his closet was filled with yellow shirts? And when Elvis came to Buffalo, the Riverside Men's Shop fitted him for his purchase- a yellow suit to be worn to the Elvis concert. I think, today, Tom owns every Elvis song- and, on records, 8-tracks, cassettes and CDs

Why had he begun to drag his foot? Why did he begin to have seizures? Oh, there would be a medical diagnosis- tumor on the brain...inoperable. His response to the news was to give away his clothes and possessions to his twin. But although the chart of life said "not yet", it offered Tom another crisis. His wife of a year lost her battle with leukemia. Her parting gift to our Big Tom was a son, Tommy.

Yesterday- Fathers' Day- I visited Tom with my gift of donut holes. He looked up from his wheel chair, traces of food on his chest and lips, skin darkened by the sun he loved to bathe in. He responded to my call for a hug lifting his weakened l right arm to offer a hug. The years have not been kind to Big Tom. He has suffered great diminishment.

Yet there is still good reason to call Tom "Big". He is the one who has had to face so many physical challenges and, in his own way, to be the champ. He pecks out a message on his special computer and he smiles as we listen to the programmed message, the high tech voice speaking for him, "I pray to be healed".

Tom is "Big". A long time ago he refused to be nicknamed Tommy. Maybe that was his soul realizing that he was being called to something bigger. That unknown life script would demand the approach of someone kind of larger than life, someone who would endure with a smile, our Big Tom.

Who was this man named Saul? Those who heard the name sometimes found themselves subject to his persecutions. His reputation made him the one to be feared, the champ against the disciples of the Jew called the Christ, the one trying to destroy the Church.

But what's in a name? What changed when Saul became known as Paul? Did he become less brave? The work of God on this man's soul did not erase the warrior within. But what happened on the Road to Damascus was life changing. Saul or Paul, there was a new life script not announced via a computerized voice but offered in the words of God who said, "I will show him what he will have to suffer for my name".

Paul retold his encounter with Jesus on that road many times, an event that called him to something bigger. Once more Saul-Paul would be bold, yet without seeming to be the victor. His was a new strength served with humility, tears, trials and hardships.

I sense a smile on his face as his prayer echoes in the words to the Corinthians:

"We know that if our earthly dwelling, a tent, should be destroyed, we have a building from God...eternal in Heaven...who has given us the Spirit as a first installment".

What's in a name? The One who knew us in our mother's womb, the One who called us by name before we were born- Tom, Big Tom... Saul, Paul.

What's in a name? He knows.

CAT-CHY

Although I am not a pet person, admittedly I had two dogs in my life-Chubby when I was 9 and Tawny when I was 17. Their names help recall their descriptions but do not say anything about my relationship with these pets. Chubby, a fluffy white Spaniel-Spitz was named for his size and shape. On the other hand, Tawny was named for his color, a soft brown with tint of red. He probably was a mixed variety that revealed touches of his wolf ancestry. That's it. Did we have a person-pet relationship? What ever happened to these animals?

One day, my nephew Tommy shared his heartbreaking news that CAT his black cat pet of twelve years had to be put away. Tommy's decision was made to relieve her from the illness that was consuming her. At first, I responded with a nonchalant, "I'm sorry, guess you did the right thing." This did not match the emotion of my nephew, the friend who was experiencing loss, loss of the pet who was a part of his life and his home experience.

Cats entered my experience, not as my pet but Irene's. Irene was Tommy's Mom. Irene had a cat. After Irene and my brother were married they lived in our home and so did the cat. It was then that I was able to observe this feline and its ways and the shared companionship of person and pet. Now, everything I observed was tainted by one action which I found repulsive. When Irene was pregnant, the cat would hop on this proud mom-to-be's stomach and start kneading. Why did this bother me? Perhaps it seemed as though the cat wanted to be part of what lay in the womb of expectancy. I cannot really say except that it did.

Shortly after Tommy's birth, his mom passed away. Things would change all around us as death left its mark on all. But in the midst of this changing environment, there was the cat. I wonder if cats have sorrow and feel loss. The cat continued to do its cat things. And one, jumping up on to Tommy's crib, and kneading on the six pound baby's body, made me shoo it away. After all, this was a baby and what else might the cat do.

The cat stayed on. When the baby grew into a searching toddler, my dad would make toys on strings to lure the cat into playful times with the playful toddler. And so a child's relationship with the cat deepened. Whatever happened to that cat?

When Tommy was six, there no longer was a cat in the house. Since I would be leaving, I decided to buy him a gift. Yes, the gift was a kitten. The history of that kitten and its six year old friend is obscured by the years. What is certain is that that youngster would cherish the friendship of cats throughout his life.

As I reflected on the episode of cat pets in our household, Tommy's recent loss emerged as a very serious loss, a bereavement of one who had lost a friend. Yet, a greater loss overshadows that event, the death of a mother those many years ago, a birth mother to care for him, nurture and embrace him, and yes, a mom to introduce him to her own friendly, loving spirit and the comfort and delight of having a pet kitten.

What am I missing? The love connection of a young mother with her husband and a motherless child's developing love for his father.

I look back at Irene's cat friend and love and Tommy's life, his relationship with cats and his father and, I think a mom and a son, it must have been catchy.

His father was a carpenter and he grew up knowing about wood. We can imagine this father teaching his son, showing him how to handle wood- this object of their daily work. We can picture Joseph and Jesus working together, Joseph placing Jesus' hands on each piece of wood, gently forming the crude wood into beautiful household furniture or everyday tools, gently forming a relationship. They say, "The apple does not fall far from the tree." Father and Son would share their work and life. Jesus would suffer the loss of Joseph one day. He would lose a father, friend and teacher. He would feel the suffering of loss. There remains the relationship of the man, the carpenter, to his wood and the son who would experience his own relationship to the wood.

Once more, Jesus lifts up the wood, this time to bear its weight, its crude form, on his shoulders. A mother watches as his hands touch the wood, this time roughly, forced against its grain. This carpenter now becomes the object, hung high in the place where death is the price of love. As we look upon this gift to and for us, we grieve and we hear Jesus' words, "When you see me, you see the Father, the Father and I are one."

I cannot help but ponder that as I see Tommy in his loss, indeed in his life, that cats are his wood of relationship, that the son now resembles the mother, that the apple does not fall far from the tree.

Father and son would share their work and life. Jesus would suffer the loss of Joseph one day. He would lose a father, friend and teacher. He would feel the suffering of loss. There remains the relationship of the man, the carpenter, to his wood and the son who would experience his own relationship to the wood.

Once more, Jesus lifts up the wood, this time to bear its weight, its crude form, on his shoulders. A mother watches her son, now grown, and remembers the boy carpenter. She watches as his hands touch the wood, this time roughly, forced against its grain. This carpenter now becomes the object, hung high in the place where death is the price of love.

As we look upon this gift to and for us, we grieve and we ponder Jesus' words, "When you see me, you see the Father, the Father and I are One". I cannot help but reflect that as I see Tommy in his loss, indeed in his adult life, that cats symbolize his wood of relationship, that the son now in a special relationship of love of his father, fully resembles the mother, that the apple does not fall far from the tree.

THE PENKSON MELODY RAMBLERS

A Family affair! The boys from Pennsylvania shared common interest- music. Five brothers grew up and moved from their coal town origins to Buffalo. Each lived a life expressing his individual vocation choice to earn a living and his after work avocation including music.

One among them, Joseph, the youngest, spent a life teaching and playing music. It was this passion that likely spurred on his older siblings to pick up their instruments and join him as "The Penkson Melody Ramblers". The name Penkson defined the group- the Penksa Sons, and each son defined his instrument- Joe (Doc) on the accordion, Michael (Mac) on the sax and twin Tony on the drums, John on the banjo. It was a family affair! Strains of their music flowed through Buffalo where weddings became their popular venue and local radio sent out their sound each week. But the tempo soon slowed down, leaving Joseph to a career teaching music and the brothers to playing at family gatherings.

A family affair? In the third grade, I was ready to make my musical debut. At our house, one could find a saxophone, guitar, violin and piano- each instrument mastered by Mac, my dad. And mom, mom played a spirited harmonica and tapped her snare drum with gusto at summer parades as she had done since a youth. Her own brother joined them- fiddle, harmonica, guitar and Saturday country music! All this in the family! What would I choose?

The violin! However, there was a definite problem, one that affected my music career. In fact, my role as musician began and ended in about three lessons. It was an ugly black, wooden violin case that became my nemesis. I was not allowed to rent an instrument so I was bound to carry it in this case. In tandem, the teacher told me to have my father repair a violin string before continuing and this third grader noticed the nice leather cases of the other children. What to do? If I didn't tell my dad about the needed repair…?

But, I am talking about a family thing. What of my siblings? Was I a model for them? On the quitter side: Mickey and the accordion, Tom and the sax. Aha! A winner- number two sibling, Sonny, followed our mom. He picked up his drum sticks and played with a Marine Corps unit and even strummed at his own wedding and later with a group at other weddings.

There was even an earlier strain from that generation proclaiming its family gift- a band led by another Joseph. Cousin Joey banged away on the washboard and played a gallon jug, harmonica and whistled in between it all. That was his sort of comedy shtick which he performed with a small group. Uncle Joe, the Ramblers leader also taught nephew Joey how to play the accordion, which he played fairly well. Joey was a real comedian and enjoyed a good laugh. Later there emerged a third generation guitar player who went from classical Penksa to charismatic praise music. Again, a drifter from the tradition. Now, we're looking into the fourth generation and a couple of piano players. Will the Ramblers revive?

My food is to do the will of the One who sent me and to complete his work...The Son "can only do what he sees the Father doing"... For everything there is a season. A family name. A family work. I look with pride at the boys who brought their music gifts into a symphony of a generation- for the public and for family appreciation too. I lament the lack of followers from among the branches of our tree. Was it non-talent or non-commitment that cut short the Rambler strain? There was a time for music and a time for no music. For everything there is a season. Now, we need to look around and see the beautiful buds that flower on our family tree...and appreciate the new season.

The words of a song flow- "I have decided to follow Jesus..." This is our real family song and there is no turning back. Our family song, our Christian song, shared in a posture of praise!

The one we choose to follow offered the words, the lyrics of his song: 'Whatever the Father does, the Son does too." What a deep and penetrating commitment of Jesus! He does the work of the Father and never reneges, never quits. Rather he picks up the cross and teaches us the "family" way:

He creates an enduring family: "mother, here is your son; son, here is your mother". He shows faithfulness to God, forgiveness to those who offend us, love as he has loved... This is the message for all generations, a tradition for his family, our family. It becomes the symphony that preserves the work of the Father and of the Son. A family affair, now my generation song to play, using the gifts given me by my God while relying on the strains of grace from above.

HELLO AGAIN!

Ellicott Creek Park! A great place for a picnic, to gather with family to celebrate my entering the Grey Nuns. Yes, and a time to say goodbye, at least for a while.

Even as I was about to be offering that goodbye, I had the wonderful experience of a "hello again", of spending time with my cousin Bob. Bob, seven years older than I. Bob with whom I had lived and shared childhood experiences in the family home on North Marion Street. Bob, whose life and mine took other paths over the years. This "hello again" continued in his home and late into the wee hours. Surely other picnickers were already in their homes and in their beds and perhaps starting to wake to a new day.

That overnighter with Bob was a time of catch up, of sharing childhood memories, his married family life and childen, the theology of religious life, our grownup hopes and topics like, "What's the difference between a nun and a sister?. It was a time for hearing his growing family story, of being in touch with his wife again, and his two girls whom I had never met

Another goodbye as I left Bob's home, a goodbye that I never expected to be the last. Could tears flush away all the other old memories? I remember calling out to a disbelieving Bob, "Santa is coming to our door. Come on Bob!" Or, Bob who did not accept his little cousin's defense when she presented him the licked down ice cream cone with the admission, "yours was melting, mine wasn't". When Bob grew up to be a sailor, I was proud of my older cousin who was handsome in his Navy whites. Always a bit of a philosopher, he recognized the right way! "I don't put seat covers on the seats until they are worn down. Why cover what is new and nice looking?" Or, even before they were required by law, Bob would pull the seat belt across his chest...even in the back seat.

The only person that died in that car accident was Bob, Bob sitting in the back seat, the safety item strapped across his now crushed chest. Now the reality set in as I said a final, "Goodbye Bob"!

Goodbye Bob, but, I will remember you because when you were here

31

and with me as a child our lives were intermeshed. I will picture the family Sunday visits that gradually felt a separation- you growing into a teen, from me your little girl cousin. You married and we began to drift apart as we followed new commitments, responded to new calls in life.

My heart is filled with memories but most of all that we met to say hello again that picnic day and had time to share them. Yes, we said goodbye, and goodbye.

Goodbyes are difficult when we say them with such finality. Yet we are consoled by scripture when we listen to Jesus speaking to his Apostles, words of farewell, His goodbye. He speaks of all that they had experienced of Jesus, of the love and friendship he had shared with them. It was a time to recall all that they knew about Jesus, to spend time catching up, as it were. Finally, Jesus makes a promise, the coming of an Advocate, the Holy Spirit to remind them about their relationship and all that they shared together and on that day.

The walk to Emmaus found disciples remembering. Disappointed disciples, mourning the death of Jesus, remembering their days with him! When an unrecognized Jesus met them on the way, he encouraged their understanding of scriptures. Then in the experience of sharing bread they became aware of his presence. Once more a hello, one that emerged at table and they rushed to share the message of the Risen Jesus with the Apostles.

I think that all that happened in life between cousins and that time of goodbye have not drifted into nothingness. Rather, we too remain in communion because we remember, because there is a spirit that binds us and there is a place prepared for us where Bob and I will meet to say, "Hello" again.

MICHAEL'S DREAM

When I visited my mom that Sunday, I encouraged her with thoughts of Michael's wedding the next Saturday. From her closet, I brought her two items of clothing. "Which do you want to wear? I asked. The choice made, I lifted up a pearl necklace and suggested it was a good match. Mom was now set for the celebration.

But, the next day, Monday, a call came with the news: "Your mother died during the night." The chosen blue suit and pearls would now be worn for a different celebration- the life of Sophie Urbaniak Penksa. It began with the wake, where relatives and friends remembered the woman, her life, and shared loving stories. Then, at Holy Mass, the celebration highlighted her Baptism, her life of faith and being clothed in the white garment that marked her new life in Christ. It was during this time of remembering and story telling that Michael, mom's fourth grandson, cautiously offered, "I had a dream about gram the night that she died".

"The dream story began with Michael and Kathy, his wife to be, who were driving in the Riverside area. Because they were near gram's, they decided to stop in for a quick visit. You need to know that Michael's visits were usually on holidays and an impulsive stop was unusual. When the two rang the bell, Grandma, who had lost both legs some years before, stood up and walked to the door to greet the visitors. "I am sorry, Michael, I won't be able to come to your wedding," she said.

I tell and re-tell this dream story with the same wonder, the same chills running down my arms with each re-telling. And, the point of it? It seems to reinforce a belief in the mystery that life doesn't come to an end, that it just changes. Even the change doesn't suggest an end. The dream becomes a channel, perhaps in a way that Email or Imail carry messages through space, and two people are able to communicate. The dream makes real the mystery of the communication that exists between what we have called two worlds, that of the living and the dead. Or, better said, communication between two beings the living and the living!

I reflect on other dreamers- Pharaoh, Samuel, Pilot's wife... And, Joseph to whom God spoke in a dream.

What is the truth about dreams? Noticeably, the biblical characters who have dreams do not dismiss them but seem to search for their meaning or to act at once in obedience to the dream message. The dreams that emerge from the scriptures do not cause us concern, or surprise us, and we accept the way characters respond to them. But what of Michael's dream? The characters involved are real. Their relationship, while plausible, is not usual. Yet, there is a relationship, an accepted invitation that must not be broken.

As I ponder the dream and search for meaning, the obvious is in mom's words, "Sorry, I cannot come to your wedding." For me, the mystery is that it is Michael who conveys the dream to us. Michael is the receiver and the final transmitter of the message. Is it the spoken message that matters? Or, should one's interest focus on the people? I focus on Mom. Mom rises from the chair and walks toward Michael to give him her message. She walks. Mom, who suffered the loss of legs some years earlier. Mom who suffered an immobilizing stroke thirty years before. Mom rises and walks. Our faith teaches that in our resurrection with Christ all will be made new. We live in the hope of a perfect, resurrected body. This body will imitate Jesus' in his appearances to his disciples: uninhibited by doors and suddenly appearing in their presence. Was Michael's dream a confirmation of our faith and hope in the resurrection?

THE WILD BLUE YONDER

Where is heaven? Someplace beyond the wild blue yonder, in the sky someplace out there? I think heaven is a definite place, the place in God's presence promised to us. Whatever it's name or wherever it is, that's where Butchie is now.

I was invited to remember my cousin, to say the words that told a memory of his history, briefly capturing moments, to those who sat before me mourning the loss of husband, father, to his relatives, friends and associates. Yes, those who shared at least a season of association with him!

And so I reflected: "About Butchie"

I have some thoughts I want to share.
They're all about someone for whom we care.
And you may call him John while I say Butchie.
Now God did say of him and you and me...
'Twas I who formed you and called you by name
So the one we love is really the same.

Childhood memory goes to 118 Pine and Sunday visits there.
As kids with Butch My brothers Sonny, Mick and Tom found things to share.
Four would huddle, Sears Catalog in hand, eyes on pictures of gals in scant underwear.
Now Kay and Bob and I, we'd just stay apart.
Kay with dolls and toys, Bob with study and me doing art.

Art, that's a talent Butch would later show.
At Butchie's, cakes and goodies were homemade you know....
But when Butchie was at our house, he looked for stale.
"Got some old, store cupcakes?" he'd wail.

Butchie had Smokey his cat and airplanes to fly.
We didn't know then he'd be an airman bye and bye
Nor did we know then he'd grow into John
And take up mechanics and an air force uniform don.

But first he wore the sign of faith- "Take and Eat" said his God.
He lived God's lessons- all Ten, and God was giving him his nod.
Dating and falling in love were John's thing.
For Butch- now as John- marriage was more than a ring.

Was it Butchie or John that knew important things like being loyal?
'Cause faithful husband, proud father too, in love for them he'd live to toil.
A man of memories he, perhaps a pack-rat on the side.
Husbanding, fathering, serving the USA, these three and his faith his pride.

His life was full and the path was a test.
But God was with him loving, forgiving, when he came to rest.
I hope tho, John didn't find the gate unhinged, try to fix it and get in late.
Today, amid our tears there's joy as we pause to ponder....
See ya later Butchie, John...in that place above- Your Wild Blue Yonder.

Yes, the words flowed. Tears, and chuckles, memories, accompanied the listening.

Perhaps too, a memory of the Jesus story. Many have wondered about the boy Jesus and just what kind of boy he was. Myths arise about Jesus performing miracles like restoring life to a dove. Scripture says little about the boy but how, at twelve, he slipped away from his parents to meet and talk with Jewish scholars.

Likely, at home, Jesus was learning the trade of his father and his reading was a catalog too- of testaments, stories of his ancestors and their God. He would emerge from boyhood and accept the adult role as Son of the Father. He would accept its challenges, loyal to the mission of being about his Father's business.

In the end, from the cross, he would acknowledge those who shared his journey, Mary his mother, his disciple John. As he stretched out his arms of salvation he would even invite another, our Butchie, to share with him his wild blue yonder.

A LIFE CYCLE

There are cousins we remember from family visits as kids. They are part of a tradition of family get-togethers on Sundays- the time set aside, not for shopping or laundering or other tasks- the day called holy by command: "Thou shall keep holy the Lord's day.

So it was with the Szuflewski and Penksa families. Visits, times for us to know each other well and to share the joys and intimacies of each family! In one such time, Bernice became a special part of our Penksa life; Bernice, the younger of the two girls.

It is in this setting that I remember Bernice and her famous motorcycle ride with Roger. Out of that first ride would come the tale of a life time. And fifty years later, for a wedding anniversary, I chronicled the Bernice and Roger story with a poem of remembering.

Roger and Bernice

You came together so long ago
I remember as you rode side by side
A motorcycle ride, you teen-friends on the go
Soon horizons would open wide

You've lived together now for many a year
I see you living faithful side by side
A marriage blessed, yours a holy career
Day to day your love ne'er denied

You brought new life, 'twas God's plan
I see you with children at your side
A family large, yours a growing clan
Always embracing them, a love spread wide

You come now to celebrate your vowed life
I pray in gratitude for the "ride" you've taken
A lifetime continues, your friendship as man and wife
Today, your story, a witness of love unshaken

So what joy do I offer on your anniversary day?

I'm happy to pause and with you take a look
A life portrait created and baby pictures display
You've come a long way in creating a beautiful Hoeltke book

Oh, and **Happy Anniversary Day!**

With Love, Cousin Ruthy

Scripture tells us that Mary went to visit her cousin Elizabeth. Surely she did not just knock at the door, share a meal and travel the long distance home. We can imagine who they became for each other- one assisting the other, spending time together. More likely Elizabeth, who was much older, was really Mary's aunt. Her aunt, wizened by age and experience, opened not only her door but her heart to the younger Mary. In the openness of that home the young Mary would find the comfort and consolation, perhaps not offered by her community back in Nazareth. And when it was time, we find Mary joined with Joseph on the road to Bethlehem, to the place where the Child would be born.

How many times has a "cousin" knocked at our door? How many times have we "Elizabeths" opened the door and embraced the visitor? In that embrace have we recognized the presence of Jesus, perhaps hidden-visible only in the need of the visitor?

We might cry out to the Lord: When did I see you hungry or homeless, alone or in whatever need...? And, Jesus will remind us: whenever you did it to one of your "cousins" you did it to me.

A SENSE OF HUMOR

A knock at the door of my third period Freshman Spanish class! In walked James, age eight, a tyke from the grade school just across the hockey field. He came bearing a note from Sister Mary. In part it read "he doesn't believe Jesus laughed either".

But, what was this all about? I had earned the reputation among my sister nuns of saying that Jesus never laughed. Oh, they tried the same arguments that now I placed on this eight year old. I think that Jesus must have laughed when Peter tried walking on the water and then fell in! Or, didn't he find it funny when that short guy, Zaccheus, was up in a tree? Or, when he called the rich guy a fool for building a storage barn, did he laugh at such a dumb thing to do because he'd be dead the same day!

The devil's advocate in me passed over this little boy perhaps because he clung to a strict black Baptist culture. But I was white and Catholic. What would prompt me to say "I don't believe Jesus laughed"?

The answer, a sense of humor! Perhaps that element was lost on those who heard my admission. Did they believe me? Was my humor so hidden or did they just enjoy a humorous bout with this apparently senseless sister nun of theirs? Nevertheless even today, so many years later, they often greet me with a challenge of my "belief". I have never admitted a change of that belief.

Hidden under all of this is my history of humor. Actually, I think it is associated with my DNA. Despite the many and varied emotions expressed in our family relationships, humor often emerged. Sometimes it was in the form of puns or funny lines or reactions to situations.

My dad, called by his best friend "the funniest man I know", walloped us with puns. Oh, oh…another "Mack" joke we'd claim in his name! On a bright sunny Sunday, he would look out the window and we could mouth the pun as he proclaimed "We're going to a Christening today… Buffalo had a little son". He would say of his barber who had little to trim, "he told me my hair is coming out nicely".

And mom, she had some favorite lines like "sonofabetcha thought I was gonna swear". Who laughs when punishing a mouthy child? Mom walloped me with an old broom as I tried to escape her. The broom broke against my shoulder and mom broke into laughter. Even when mom was in her worst health, living with a debilitating stroke, having lost both legs…at Christmas she lamented "no one bought me slippers".

So, how about Jesus? Was I wrong to think, or perhaps pretend to believe, that he never laughed or didn't have a sense of humor? I think of the poster picture of Jesus, a black and white sketch, head thrown back in a facial posture of laughter, appropriately called "The Laughing Jesus".

––––––––––––––

What of the Jesus of the Scriptures? There are no places that represent him as the black and white picture. Indeed everything about Jesus wasn't simply "black and white". We hear that the writers each captured a picture of Jesus familiar to him and four pictures emerge as Gospels.

We are taught about the humanity of Jesus. The Gospels offer descriptive assurance of human traits. He cried at the death of a friend, Lazarus. He sympathized with the needs of the suffering- the blind, the crippled and healed them. When it was time for a break he was aware of a hungry crowd and provided them with a supper of bread and fish. We see him at a wedding celebration where wine was served and at homes of friends like Martha where he was invited to meals. He had a welcoming affection for children and could display anger at the actions of some adults. Finally, Jesus felt the pangs of bodily suffering, the pain of nails pounded into his flesh and he even cried out to his Father.

Human! But humorous? He was like us in all things but sin. Why are the Gospel writers quiet about that human trait, laughter that distinguishes us from the brute? Did Jesus laugh? have a sense of humor? Finally, what do I really believe is the answer?

Well, I have a sense of humor. But the answer to that question is questionable.

Yardley Beckons
Sense and Nun-sense

The perennial questions: "Why did you want to become a nun?" or "How did you know you had a call to be a nun?" The response to each is difficult, not something so clear cut.

And, once the step is taken, discernment between the congregation and the sister to be can be filled with challenges. Here's a peek into some of those challenges.

BECOMING GREY

When I started out toward Yardley Pa. to take on becoming a nun (actually a postulant), an entourage of family and friends had bid me well. I was departing this place, Buffalo, where I had spent all the years of my life.

Fifteen potential "Greys" arrived at the Motherhouse on Quarry Road where Grey Nuns, professed and novices alike, formed a long (Grey) line to share their traditional welcome wish- "perseverance". Once we had accepted the perseverance greeting from the professed Greys, there was to be no more social consorting with them. We must pass them by with a hospitable nod of the head.

And so I moved into this new environment, moved into my new life style. It would be a time of revelation: What really goes on in a convent!

We were introduced to "what goes on" very quickly. There were new clothes, a shared bedroom with special regulations for its care, a new hour for going to bed and for rising, assigned chores (and unexpected ones) and classes, new ways to eat oranges and bananas, regulated times for talking and for being silent. . There was a prayer schedule, new forms of prayer with appropriate posture for each; and every so often these were accompanied by mistakes and giggles. There were the two great hours of the day- sewing during sacred silence and "forced fun"- that time when one was expected to be present with the group and to enjoy oneself and each other.

We learned a new vocabulary too:
Perseverance- meant for better or worse
Doyen- referred to the oldest postulant (which title I inherited).
Benjamin- the youngest postulant
The Door Swings Open Both Ways- suggested that we'd better shape up or ship out.
Collation- the snack in-between meals.
Custody of the Eyes- no peeking at envelopes, etc. that did not apply to you.
Silence- no talking.

Grand Silence- the silence between bedtime (9pm) and breakfast the next morning

Charges- daily menial tasks.

Instruction- total immersion in learning about the vows, the Foundress, the Church (and whatever else fit in).

The Grey Nun Walk- meant hands never dropped below the waist and never rested in pockets.

Apron- that stripped cover-all, held on by two pins, appropriate for wear whenever in the dining room (just in case one was to take something to eat).

Obedience- the act of confessing a fault or receiving permission to keep or toss any item like clothes.

"Sister, Don't You Think..."- a not so obvious call to obey.

We were introduced to a common life day. Beginning at a 5:30 am rising and the multi-active schedule: Morning prayer, Mass, breakfast, charges, classes, Rosary and particular Examen, lunch, after meal charges, more classes, afternoon Instruction, dinner, after meal charges, obedience and, finally, recreation followed by lights out at 9 pm. Someplace in this day we "fit in" the traditional Grey Nun devotions and meditation. Oh, one might have taken collation mid-afternoon or before retiring (and always with apron on). Wow! Having completed college, however, I was also assigned to do some library work. I was also able to find some extra time during this schedule for a game of table tennis.

Very simple, once you get the hang of things! It is thus that the new life began.

The Apostles were gathered in the Upper Room. Something was about to happen that would inspire them into a new life, a Spirit filled life.

Yet, when each first met Jesus and accepted his invitation, there was no formal script about what life would be like. They responded and moved into a new life style. As they walked with Jesus they were introduced to the faith challenges demanded of them. They would experience a new understanding of the Sabbath, a definition of who is one's neighbor, learn about inclusion, participate in the feeding thousands with a few fish, and witness the raising of Jesus' friend. On the other hand, this new walk tested them with moments of doubt, betrayal, and even denial.

Twelve disciples were in that Upper Room, novices readied, even with uncertainty, to take on the role of Apostle, to face new challenges. Their response to the fire of the Spirit became the fire of perseverance, the fire that would consume the world with new life- the Christian message, the Church- into the centuries that lay ahead.

"BREAK A LEG"

There is an old saying known best by theater folks- "break a leg!" The adage is pronounced heartily as a good luck wish to the actor as he moves toward a role on stage. No one ever said "break a leg" when I started out toward the Grey Nun Motherhouse to take on the role of postulant.

The only words that I carried with me, other than tearful ones that accompany separation, were the concerns of Aunt Frances. "You won't be able to ski anymore; they will put you to work in the fields; you won't be able to do all the fun things you've been doing at home. Didn't Aunt Frances know that I was the worst skier on the beginner slope? That I had a plaque to prove it? That crutches had been part of that experience? And, the fields...well, that is another tale to be told. Actually, I had my own "won't list", the important things that I would miss: drinking my favorite beverage- coke, wearing my Wigwam wool socks ($1 a pair) and sporting around in jeans (in my day called dungarees). Not a particularly interesting list of misses!

At the Motherhouse, I found that it was not all work and prayer and no physical activity or play. There was walking. This activity was a common one and was often accompanied by recitation of the Rosary, alone or with another. Then there was postulant-pinochle, also a "community" experience. I was often enticed into this activity by Roselee, who sought escape from her frequent toothaches. Her "Ruth, my tooth" was an irresistible call to the table. I joined the more athletic in the group who indulged in indoor table tennis or outdoor basketball. I found myself enjoying these more physical activities.

At the same time, I was experiencing some difficulty walking. Mornings found me limping to the bathroom. Was the chronic pain in my legs a signal of a minor basketball injury? Or, as I suspected, was it simply a syndrome left over from pre-postulant days when wearing high heels daily on concrete based floors left me with a condition called spurs? No matter the name, the pain continued. One morning as I was painfully walking up the stairs, a cheery novice offered the expected greeting: "Good morning, how are you?" The answer, "I am in pain", was unexpected, I could tell, after her uncertain, "oh" as she continued on her way. Only much later would she recall the meeting on the stairs! Not long after, it would be a more somber invitation by the Mistress of Postulants, Sister Daniel Marie, "I think you had better see the doctor about your pain". In the convent, words like "I think" really had a meaning not yet understood by an independent minded, adult, postulant. Translated properly they had to do with obedience. So it was that I made a visit to the doctor and returned with no definite prognosis. Before the day was over there was a phone call with the message retold by D.M. (a pithy but affectionate nickname for our postulant mistress): "You must go to the hospital tomorrow because the x-ray seems to reveal that you are walking on two broken legs." And it was the evening and morning before the trip to the hospital and the schedule went on as usual.

Julia, another postulant, was my companion on the journey. There is an irony yet to be fulfilled, later to be explained, about our making this jaunt to the hospital together. After a brief examination, the doctor said he had bad news for me. My immediate response to bad news was the dreaded thought- cancer. "Put on your shoes", he instructed, "and follow me". "You have two broken legs. Now, how could that be bad news? Bad news is cancer. I returned to the Motherhouse donned in one walking cast, with crutches and a wheel chair for mobility during the next nine weeks.

Thus it was that that I "walked" onto this new stage of my life. Well wishers never did say "Break a leg" for the role I was taking on. The word had been "perseverance!"

Why do bad things happen to good people? The question looms; it rises out of our often thoughtless despair. The people observing the man born blind questioned whether it was his sin or those of his parents that were the cause of his affliction. When Jesus cured him he jumped about, calling: "I only know that I was blind and now I can see!" as he recognized, by this new sight, the people and things about him.

Perhaps, too, he reflected on how they had cared for him as he went about his daily life. Theirs was a shared life of perseverance, of living out the things that came their way. I suspect that they experienced each other's frailties and perhaps bonded in unexpected ways. Was theirs despair or was there room in this blindness for the unexpected gift of light, of recognition, of meeting each other in new ways?

In my infirmity, I became dependent on fourteen postulants. The natural separation by our ages, eighteen to thirty three, was dissipated by a wave of community born in our perseverance....together. In bad moments shared, we realized that we were good people who had become the "Friendly Fifteen."

RED WINE AND WHITE SPREAD

It was a fast day- Holy Thursday. It was a work day in the Library. Rosalie and I spent the day in the workroom where we marked books. In those days books were identified by the Dewey decimal system and the appropriate numbers were hand marked on the spine of the books. Rosalie would clean the spines and I would perform the art of marking them. This would be followed by spray adhesive to keep this Dewey deco from rubbing off.

I learned the art of book marking while a student at d'Youville College. Part of our freshman orientation was a period of time learning how to use the library. A test revealed that my skills in library use were deficient. The librarian was a portly Sister Ruth with as wide and generous a spirit. She advised me: "You do not know much about the library but your printing is impressive" (I had chosen to print rather than write the test). Thus it was that I was introduced to the library workroom and the artful task of putting the Dewey numbers on the spines of books.

On this particular holy day in the Novitiate, Rosalie and I had worked without any sustenance and in the silence required of the holy day. Rosalie was the one more apt to keep the silence as diligently as she performed her tasks. I suppose the silence was getting to me. Or maybe it was Rosalie being so serious and attentive to her work that tempted the teaser in me. I began to sniff the fumes of the adhesive spray knowing that she would be annoyed by this bad behavior. In her loudest whisper accompanied by an intense glare she gave me a slap on the hand ordering me to obedience- "cut it out". I laughed as I engaged her temper.

We left the library looking forward to a dinner to break the fast. While we were working in the library, others were preparing the table in the common room.

This room and this table knew a variety of activities. It was the room where we learned to pray the Office of Our Lady in monastic style. Seated on chairs lined up on either side of the long table allowed us to alternate chanting the lines of the psalms. This room and this table provided the setting for an hour of recreation (affectionately called "forced fun") each evening. This room and this table invited us to hang out between classes or other activities, to allow card players to gather. Today, they would be transformed into a banquet space and table with Novices gathered to celebrate the feast.

We entered the room noticing the table of celebration. Everything looked lovely. The old wooden table was hidden under a beautiful white cloth, and place settings were the promise of the meal to come.

"And, Mary Liz's family sent this red wine", a Novice chimed as she poured the deep red-purple liquid into each empty glass. I don't know why it attracted me, a non-drinker, but I said that I would like to try some. And, try it I did, not as one accustomed to sipping wine, but as a coca cola guzzler. The drink slipped easily and tastefully past my palate and into my empty stomach. "Another, I'd like another". The second glass was consumed in a similar fast gulp. I chuckled as I admitted how good the wine was. Then the chuckle changed into an uncontrollable series of giggles. Had the earlier sniffs of adhesive spray added to the effect of red wine? The Novices tried to hush me and my sounds from discovery by the Mistress. When their "shushes" had no effect, they resorted to another beverage- black coffee. Finally, their only remaining tactic was to get me to lie down. They ushered me toward my room which was next to this common room. The bed was inviting as I hopped on top of the white spread, on hands and knees, fully clothed. It was then that the Mistress appeared. "Don't you think you should undress", she suggested. It was not a question but I responded as though it were, "Oh no, this is just fine." Again, the suggestion, and again, the certain response.

What was the conclusion to doing the forbidden- lying atop one's white spread, fully clothed, and yes, full of red wine? I must confess a lack of memory. Yet there is one lingering thought. I seem to remember a smile on the Mistress's face as she repeated her subtle command to an unreasoning Canonical novice.

For sure, I have no memory of the meal that was served that evening or if I shared in it at all. But, my experience of the red wine and white spread and a smiling Mother Ann Rita, is indelibly marked in my novitiate memories.

It was a celebration, a wedding feast. The steward was confronted with guests who had, one might think, "guzzled down" the wine served them even before the party was over. Prompted by Mary, Jesus provided the second round of wine, this better than that served earlier. Picture the steward whose anxiety must have been replaced by a smile as the guests enjoyed the new supply. Do you suppose they giggled a bit as they lifted their cups again?

At another table, with his friends gathered, Jesus hosted the Jewish Passover. The place an upper room, the table set for a meal. There was wine. No need here to begin with water. Jesus passed the cup. The taste of wine warmed their palate and entered their stomach. Their real emptiness was soothed by the release of Jesus himself into their being. Giggles? No. Instead the warmth of Presence, a transforming moment as they leaned on a table covered with a cloth, set for this particular meal, each lifting up the cup of salvation.

My sampling of the wine caught me unawares. I savored something tasty and the experience surprised me, changed me for a while. Surely the steward and guests at the wedding, and those who drank with Jesus at the Passover meal, were caught up in the experience of Jesus. Our encounters with Jesus have in them something of the unexpected.

Why wine? Jesus' first miracle and his ultimate gift, both offered in this ordinary drink, provide what ordinary wine can do- change the one who drinks.

THOU SHALT NOT TAKE TAXI
RIDES WITH THY MOTHER

Roselee (later to become Sr. Jane) had a toothache. Actually, her teeth troubled her frequently. Sometimes she just used that identified condition to lure me into a game of pinochle: "Ruth, my tooth!" How could I be sure? Supposedly, this activity relieved the pain. Who was I to deny her relief? Thus, I would often be drawn to the common room and a game of cards with Roselee and anyone else who responded to her hue and cry.

When the condition persisted the Mistress of Postulants saw fit to suggest that she see the dentist. Now, as was the custom, a sister never traveled alone, so Roselee selected me as her travel mate. We received an appropriate amount of money to pay for the train and bus ride to and from the dentist's office.

It happened, as we were waiting for the return bus to the train that an interesting coincidence occurred. A passing taxi stopped and a familiar voice called out. It was Roselee's mother. She offered us a ride to the train. I was delighted and eager. Roselee, however, wanting to be obedient, made a negative response to the offer. Instead, she warned me in a whisper that this was not permitted. Might "she" (the reference to the Mistress) think this was a planned meeting? Might we have to report ourselves for knowingly having a family visit at an inappropriate time? Her fears did not affect me and I encouraged taking the ride. "It's your mom", I insisted. "It is not as though it was arranged."

Roselee was silent as we rode to the train station. I provided the conversation: "We are returning from the dentist's office...Yes, Roselee will finally have some relief...Oh, things are going fine in the Novitiate... We do look forward to the upcoming visiting day...Thanks so much for the ride....It was really nice to see you...Bye bye."

Immediately, the second part of Roselee's concern surfaced- what about the fare? If we return with it "she" will know that we took that ride. Since we have the money we would have to return it which meant we would have to admit to taking the ride. ...that we participated in a family visit.

I agreed that the unused fares would add to the dilemma. The problem solver in me was activated. I took the extra money and spent it buying candy from the machine in the train station. Of course we had to eat it! Another no no. The sisters do not eat outside the dining room without permission. My mother always said that if you tell a small lie you will end up having to tell more lies. Did the digestion of the candy bars bring an end to our most dire situation?

Roselee urged my promise not to "report ourselves" or she would leave. While I thought it better to do so, I did agree. Did we ultimately do the required thing? Perhaps we did...Roselee became Sister Jane. Were there more pinochle games played? Perhaps the dentist trip served its purpose...I do not remember. But I will always remember Roselee, her teeth and our taking of the forbidden fruit- and yes, we did travel together again, many times…and often prayed: "Our Father...forgive us our trespasses..."

There was a garden called "the Novitiate". And, there was one above us called "the Mistress" who frequently cautioned us that the "door swings both ways". While our adventure to the dentist did not result in our being expelled from that garden of preparation, it was certainly a call to obedience, our call to not partake of "forbidden fruit". A test! Maybe we did not do well on taxi rides and candy bars, but unlike Adam and Eve, life would go on as usual in this garden in Yardley, Pa.

We, humans...nun-humans too, thrive on second chances. What a difference from what happened in the original Garden where death and severe change came upon the human condition, upon all creation. Yet, they, and we too, disobey and do not die forever without a second chance.

Some, by disobedience, suffer immediate physical death without a second chance. I remember eighth grade and David who rode his sled into the street. A car injury, Illness and death followed. We need to obey our parents, our employers, and be honest to the tasks entrusted to us lest we too die or are the cause of another's death without that precious second chance.

The One whom we call Father gave Adam and Eve, and us, opportunities for second chances even in view of the final punishment- physical death. In our disobedience, were we spiritually dead? ... The words echoed from the garden: "...for on the day you eat of it you must surely die."

Our sincere repentance relieves us of our sin and leads us to the confessional where Forgiveness offers us a second chance. I think that we are called to be people who offer second chances to others, to be the forgivers in the gardens of life where we find ourselves- in our homes, at our places of work or ministry, with our friends, among our acquaintances... I believe that we are to pray to forgive others as we want to be forgiven.

In the loving code of the Novitiate, where "the door swings both ways", Roselee and I knew the experience of a door that did not slam shut.

Shoes. I needed a new pair of shoes. The traditional box heeled, black "nun shoes" were no longer the absolute. It was thus that I would venture to the mall to make my purchase.

Nora came with me, honoring the tradition that sister must travel with a companion. Nora was a great companion. Her healthy humor was expressed under her other recognized name, "Marky". We talked and laughed on our little trip. The loafers, Bass-Weegens, were purchased and we started back to the Motherhouse. Soon, in the realization that we were near Goodnose, the best ice cream place in Buck's County, combined with some left over money from the shoe purchase, temptation loomed. And we submitted. What the heck! So the shoes cost a couple dollars more!

Goodnose has a selection of ice creams unmatched by any ice cream parlor. I always read the selection carefully and then choose chocolate. We licked and laughed as we headed toward Quarry Road and the Motherhouse. It was then that "Marky" emerged. "Look," she said, "it's the Mistress." I had lost my bearings and did not realize that we had not yet entered the Motherhouse property. The ice cream took a leap from my nervous hand and found rest on my grey domino (cape). A chocolate covered domino. How would I explain that?

An explanation would be necessary. There was a tradition for returning home. One did not talk to anyone at all until visiting the Superior, in this case the Mistress, and offering the greeting: "Praised Be Jesus Christ." I would have to present myself before her, with my praise, my shoes, and my chocolate domino. How could I cover up the fact that I had made an illegal purchase and then ate the product outside of the dining room, and without the striped apron? Marky was clear, but me? Hmmm.

The box. Yes, the box would be my answer. As we entered the room, I held the shoe box near to my chest, covering my crime. We offered the greeting and I quickly turned to go. "Aren't you going to show me the shoes?" Oh oh! "Why don't I just go and put them on, and then show them to you?".

Thank God for shoe boxes! The cover-up worked!

Yes, the cover-up worked. Oh, I don't believe I would have been asked to leave the convent on the basis of my indiscretion. But the Novitiate is an on trial kind of experience. It is a time and place to learn, to pray, to be strengthened to make a final commitment to live a religious life identified as a follower of Marguerite d'Youville (our Founder),

In this sense, I think of Peter whom Jesus would name "Rock" and upon whom he would build his Church. Peter's Master had known that he would fail, that he would cover-up his identity when he became afraid. "I have prayed that your faith may not fail, and once you have recovered, you in your turn must strengthen your brothers." The denials came, three times, when he covered-up his identify as a follower of Jesus. But as predicted, he recovered. He models for all of us the way we are mislead by our fears, the way we deny the Lord, and how Grace is there for us to recover.

Did I recover from my cover-up? There were more such events, I suspect. I look back at them more with humor than with serious detractions from the religious life I was called to follow. The day would come when I would make a final commitment, as did Peter, when I would accept my identity as a Grey Nun. The day would come when I too would choose the Cross as my model, not as Peter chose that Cross, in the most humble of ways, when he was arrested and marked as a follower of the Christ.

Yes, I have recovered in the deepest sense to give spiritual strength to my brothers and sisters through my ministry...but, I watch out for those little cover-ups. The devil makes me do them. Or, is it the other Markeys in my life?

AND THE HILLS WERE ALIVE WITH...

My Aunt Frances was special to me. I grew up believing her to be my God-mother. When it turned out, that she wasn't, that I didn't even know the sponsoring names on my birth certificate, it didn't seem to matter. For some reason there was a strong bond between us.

Perhaps, when my plans to be a nun were revealed, her response was the strongest because of that bond. Not strong as in, "Yes!" Rather, she predicted what she thought was wrong with my decision. Among the negative litany of reasons was her concern that "they'll put you to work in the fields doing farm work".

Now, my aunt was not psychic. Nor did her words bring a curse on me. Yet, In fact, I did do some work in the fields behind our Motherhouse. It was because I was looking for a task, something to occupy time after class, prayers, kitchen duties, and daily chore assignment. I asked because, being a college graduate, I was free from classes taken at our Junior College by younger postulants.

It was thus that I approached our Mistress requesting permission to cut grass.

I had noticed the grounds' caretakers mowing the grass. It looked like a relaxing task and I certainly enjoyed driving and the outdoors. It was an opportunity to enjoy the outdoors and take in the smell of new cut grass.

The yes to my request was accompanied by the need to speak to the maintenance men. Another yes and an assignment! I was to cut the grass in the field behind the barn. Of course if I was to cut grass I must learn to clean the mower first. So, the professionals directed this postulant in the art of keeping tools in proper working order.

I wonder how I looked in my black costume- postulant dress, veil and stockings, perched high on the huge lawn mower. It must have been a sight to see the unusually tall grass being reduced to an inch or so as I drove the vehicle through that under cared for area. And when it was done, I was proud of the clean shaven appearance left behind.

Something unusual followed that first experience. The itches! For the next two days I began to scratch and scratch. The discomfort was unbearable. Finally, I paid a visit to the doctor to find out what this strange malady was. His question included the answer. "Were you in the grass recently?" Flea bites was the diagnosis! The grassy hills behind the old barn were alive with fleas!

The decision to enter the convent was not colored by the expectations suggested by my concerned aunt. I think that when one hears the call and follows one does not conjure up a list of the odd things that might occur. Changes in life style, like personal independence, religious activities, or schedules might hold a prominent place. But, those out of the ordinary experiences cannot be foreseen decision makers. Who would have written a score with the words,"The hills are alive with the bites of fleas"?

Can you picture Jesus calling the Apostles as he walked along? Their yes was uncomplicated. They heard the call and answered, knowing and willing to leave all behind. His followers seemed to see the bigger picture, to accept the larger expectations, the change in their life style.

The"what ifs" of other days, times when they would experience unexpected personal choices, weaknesses, or times of relating to the actions of Jesus, were unpredictable. They were not a part of their initial response to his call and likely, proud to be in the company of Jesus.

Did they anticipate what might happen in those obvious moments of invitation?

"Come away with me to pray" he invited. Did they first ask themselves, "What if I fall asleep?"

"You feed them yourselves" he instructed. Did they ever think they would be asked to do such a thing as provide for the thousands, to do such a thing with so, little?

Go and prepare a Passover meal" Jesus told them. Did they first wonder if he would change their tradition?

The Gospel reminds us that there is a large picture and there are those intimate responses within the framework of our decisions

In the end, each of us can echo a tune refined by those situations; we can sing out "the hills are alive with…"

THE ENVELOPE

When I entered the convent, an aunt was worried that I would have to give up some of the activities that I enjoyed as a recent college graduate, a young active woman, a new teacher. She was certain I would just be doing heavy labor. Well, she was right that we novices did a variety of housecleaning chores, some rather heavy.

What Aunt Frances didn't anticipate was that her God-child would become a truck driver.

We had a few novices who, as college graduates, had more free time than classes, and the Motherhouse had only a few cars to accommodate their general needs. Since I was one of those with more free time, I was often called upon to do errands. And, when needed, I was the privileged driver of our small old truck.

It came to pass one day that the Superior General's Associate called upon me for help. It was an errand to the bank and, because no cars were available, I would take the old truck. She handed me the envelope containing a check to be cashed, the undisclosed amount of money to be used for airfare.

As I was about to depart, a novice suggested that, since I had the truck, I might take a bicycle to the gas station and fill the flat tires. Bicycle in the rear and envelope in hand, I began a mission that would end in a bit of mystery.

I did not know the value of the check nor did I count the cashed amount returned to me by the teller, an amount covered in the secrecy of an envelope. I tucked the treasure on the seat just under my hip and drove off to part two of my errand- the gas station. There I removed the bike, filled the tires, slipped back into the truck and was on my way home.

Back at the Motherhouse, envelope and bike properly disposed of, I went about my business. Then a page interrupted, called me to the Superior General's office. Why were there only two five dollar bills in the envelope?

After retracing the earlier journey to bank and gas station (and to anywhere near where wind might have sent the contents of the envelope), there remained no answer to what happened to the few hundred missing dollars. No answer to how all but two five dollar bills escaped the clutches of an envelope.

A woman of faith, this Associate Superior offered the reason: "Someone else needed the money more".

What happened to the money? How much was there supposed to be in that envelope I never knew or asked. I just know it was to pay for airfare to take two people to Ohio to give a Mission talk. The money had a purpose, a good purpose. The irony in this mystery is that I was one of the two sisters who was going on that Ohio Mission talk.

I think back, for a moment, to that most Holy Thursday in Christ's life, that evening when Jesus had invited his Apostles to share a Passover Meal. One guest entered with an "envelope", one filled with thirty pieces of silver. Judas knew how much was in that pouch. Judas knew the purpose of that money. But I wonder if he even knew what his real mission was.

Was Judas a man bent on serving his own need, his greed, or the needs of others? Was his mission only of what Scripture reminds us- betrayal? In some way greed, the poor and betrayal blend in an unholy alliance.

After all, he was in the company of the Apostles when Jesus was criticized for what they called the waste of money used to anoint his feet. They challenged: the money could be used for the poor, someone else might need it more. In the end, Judas became the poor. When he changed his mind about keeping the thirty pieces of silver, it was the refused money that paid for his burial in a poor man's grave. But it remains that Judas intended to point out Jesus.

How sure are we of our mission? Perhaps we have to open our envelopes and decide what to do with their contents lest some mysterious wind sweep them away,….without our knowing.

I CONFESS...

Well, this is a bold act, making a public confession that is. But outside of that hidden confessional booth, I confess that I stole a…It's bold of me to tell the tale since, by my revelation, the police might have access to an unsolved mystery.

Back in '72, I was transferred to Melrose Park in North Philadelphia. Finally, I would have the opportunity to teach Spanish again. My nun friends in the area joined me in celebrating this opportunity and our living near each other again. Our celebration was a dinner out together.

I had settled in to my new room. It was a comfortable one. Near the door was a small sink with its own glass holder built in. There was a desk near a window that faced out toward a grassy side yard. It was from out there where one could hear the firing of a gun. It was Sr. Josephine pelting the unwelcome blackbirds with sprays of bebes. But I was inside in a welcoming room that was now mine. Still, in our nun custom, if someone were looking for me, my room was identified by its last resident- "Sr. John's room", they'd say.

The dinner gathering was full of happy talk and laughter and our meals were downed with pleasure. As we began to have coffee, I remarked, "That cup is tall and narrow and would fit nicely on the glass holder on my sink". It was then that a bit of Satan entered with a temptation. "Take it they suggested". And, I yielded.

I wrapped the stolen object in a napkin and held it inconspicuously in the folds of my coat. Although easy, the theft did arouse guilt in me. As we approached the exit of the restaurant, our waitress hurried after us. "Excuse me! Excuse me! Wow! Caught! How would I handle the embarrassment of being a thieving nun? Then the dreaded question ran through my mind. Would I add lying to theft in responding to it? What does a nun or anyone do, in such a circumstance? She mouthed the question, "Did one of you…", and I cringed before she completed, "leave your glasses on the table?"

My glasses! I always took my glasses off when eating. My glasses! As I took them from her with gratitude, I never reciprocated and returned what was hers, never returned the cup- that cup that was the size and fit for my neat glass holder on my sink, in my new bedroom.

As I look back, I wonder what ever happened to that cup. I have been gifted with many cups over the years and I have worn many different pairs of glasses. One stolen cup and many cups offered as gifts. Is "I am sorry" return enough? An adequate payback!?

A random reading from Ezekiel offered consolation. There are verses about atonement: "You must celebrate the Feast of the Passover.... offered as a sacrifice for sin...for himself (oneself) and all the people".

Words away from the context of a stolen cup, but reminders. Yes, reminders of the Old and of the New Passover. It is at another table, a meal, where Jesus offers himself as a sacrifice for sin, offers the Cup of salvation, given for all. One at the meal steals as he receives the Cup. I am challenged to receive it as an atonement, to remember that this gift, this Cup joins all, one sip shared is shared with the many as I remember, "We are one Body, one Body in the Lord".

WHO'S TALKING NOW?

Five sisters filled the house car that Saturday morning. The occasion for this brief trip was to attend the Charismatic Prayer Conference being held in a local high school. Charismatic! The word spoken among many Catholics was still not appreciated. Was this something that belonged to those "born again Christians"?

I had already read about the charismatic movement. I had attended prayer meetings at Villanova, about an hour's drive from our Melrose residence. There I would avoid the greeters who hugged even strangers who were entering for the meeting. I was hug shy, raise your hands in praise shy and certainly, shy or not, unable to join the murmur of voices praying in tongues.

This Saturday I wanted to learn more about what was called tongues or prayer language. One session was for beginning information. A second was an advanced session. Because I had already read enough to understand the concept, I urged my sister companions to attend the second.

The presenters began by asking for a show of hands to see how many were new to the topic. I tugged at the sleeve of the sister sitting near me: "Don't raise your hand…I think they will suggest that those less familiar leave and attend session one." We remained, hands down, seated in the rear and watched as our three honest companions left the room. Sometimes a nun has to do what a nun has to do.

The presentation went well as we were introduced to the scriptural foundations and the notion of the Holy Spirit praying through people. The presenters even took time to pray together and then to pray in tongues among us.

Then it happened! Each presenter stood at the beginning of a row of seats. "Practice releasing to the Spirit", they instructed. "Begin to make sounds, meaningless syllables, like baby sounds. We will come down the row to pray with you."

What was I doing? I already prayed in a variety of ways. I grew up knowing how to pray the Rosary- a mantra of beads with meditations on the life of Jesus. There was my prayer book offering prayers for many intentions and situations. We prayed the Divine Office in common in our convents. I prayed along with the priest at Mass and responded to antiphonal prayers. I knew the prayer of confession, prayed the daily examen, litanies, and the familiar- "Come Holy Spirit…" What was I doing here and why?

I covered my face, as if that would avoid my having to speak to the presenter. "I am here under false pretences", I admitted as he approached me. He seemed not to care because he offered to pray with me as I uttered some meaningless words. Meaningless sounds, but my heart was begging for the action of the Spirit. Suddenly, the sounds I heard in my own voice were like a language, not like the familiar Spanish language I could speak and teach, but an unrecognizable language.

And so, the Holy Spirit listened to my heart and formed new words on my tongue. I wonder what the new language was praying. Was God listening to a scared "student", a nun wanting to get out of an embarrassing situation? Was my fearful mumbling lifted up as praise? The mystery of "tongues" remains a mystery. Yes, one can accept that the Holy Spirit comes at will to speak words of prayer in our behalf. But, the mystery is locked in exactly what the prayer may be. I suppose God knows what the prayer ought to be, for whom it might be, better than we do.

Indeed, two left that room that day. One seemed not to have received the words identified as tongues. And to be sure, when I left the room, I knew that what happened to me was God talk and not nun talk!

Now, when grace urges me and my words fail me, I will utter sounds available to the Spirit that I may speak to God…in God talk, not the words of this nun.

———————————

One of the first images I have had about "tongues" arises from the Pentecost scene when the power of God, of the Holy Spirit, appeared as tongues of fire. For the Apostles this gift empowered them to go out to the crowds and speak to them: "We hear them declaring the wonders of God in our own tongues." They were speaking in a language they did not know to minister to, to teach others. The language was, human, familiar to each who heard, words spoken by each Apostle. Theirs was the full gift of tongues, a charismatic gift!

But in the Acts of the Apostles we are assured that the Holy Spirit also falls upon us, already baptized Christians. We receive a "baptism in the Spirit" identified with more personal gifts, and often accompanied with the ability to pray in other tongues, words unfamiliar to us. We yield to the Spirit and in some unfamiliar language our prayer is lifted up to our God who takes the prayer words and distributes his grace as he wills-God's talk at work through us. No human talk here as with the Apostles with words reaching out to serve the crowds.

Have you been baptized in the Holy Spirit? I have heard the question posed many times. Unlike the disciple who admitted he had never heard there was such a thing, I can go to prayer and let a "tongue" be my answer because I experience who's talking now.

AND, WHO DO YOU SAY THAT I AM?

The question is often asked of sisters but worded another way. The question posed today: "what was your name before?"- brings back a memory. Sisters are often asked and names like Mary Joseph or John Bosco or any Mary Whomever and saint name might be offered.

The question invited me to our community room, the place where we first learned to chant the Divine Office. I can picture the long table, chairs on either side, facing forward, allowing the monastic psalmody to move from side to side as if across the church aisles.

But this day, fifteen postulants gathered to select a religious name belonging to a favorite saint or in memory of significant people. Now, chairs were facing the chalk board and names were being scribbled on the green surface.

My turn came. My first selections were nullified because older sisters already had them. So, brothers' names were scratched away- Daniel Marie, Mary Michael, St. Thomas… and my sister in law's as well- Irene Marie.

Was I being devilish or sincere when I suggested Sonny (Daniel's nick name) Marie? Still no name! Then it came and with it both a huge "no way!" enveloped in laughter. How about "Danny Thomas" I had spouted out!

We were living in the days following Vatican II. In the spirit of that document which lifted up the life we lead as baptized Catholics, we religious might also choose to keep our baptismal name. Thus, after my losing litany of names, I became Sr. Ruth Marie.

Interesting that even after the late '60s when habits were slowly disappearing, convent living was giving way to new places of ministry, old names were yielding to the one's our moms first gave us. Even over fifty years later, questions like "why don't you wear a habit?", "why are you living alone?", or "what was your name before?" still find voice among those who now enjoy the new liturgy. Wow! English not Latin!

"And you Peter, who do you say that I Am?" The question is, I think, a loaded one. The answer is in the question. But, had Peter already heard the words that echoed over the Jordan when Jesus was first identified as "my beloved Son"? Peter spurts out "You are the Messiah."

Jesus of Nazareth was his birth name. Peter was elevating the name by a description, Messiah (the Christ). For Peter, for the Jews, the Messiah should be the one to reign in glory as an earthly king, a political figure sent by God, the one who would combat their enemies.

Was Peter making a mistake? Jesus seemed not to be the expected soldier Messiah. He entered Jerusalem, not a proud conqueror on a handsome steed. Instead, he was less kingly, riding an ass. Yet, Jesus accepted who it was that Peter had called him. He said Peter was blessed for "flesh and blood has not revealed this to you". The revelation was from the Father.

Remember the "I Am"…in Jesus' question? It provoked Peter's response. Was it God, the I AM, that overpowered Peter to acknowledge Jesus as the true Messiah? People answered the question differently. But Peter? He offered in faith what in another place, an upper room, he would receive as revelation. There the Spirit would overcome him and send him to proclaim Jesus as the Savior.

Along the Way
Defining Moments in Life

Discover
Hidden Treasures

Do you think we simply drift through life? Or, is there One who helps us maneuver the course, placing before us people, events, experiences that can make a difference? Our choices are the defining moments that ultimately influence us to become who we are. Perhaps we become aware only by looking back, pausing to reflect on those moments that we experienced ...Along the Way.

I FLUNKED FIRST COMMUNION

Yes, I did "flunk" First Communion! We "publics", fourth grade children attending catechism classes, were being readied for First Communion. I remember sitting in a row near the wide classroom windows. The warm afternoon sun reached into the room and almost like a veil it covered and warmed my head. Sitting there meant I knew my prayers. Through a child's eyes and a child's pride, I was also aware of the kids on the opposite side of the room. Perhaps they weren't as prepared as I. I was a bright student, ten years old, and anxious to get on with my sacramental life. The teacher, a sister, wore a heavy brown outfit. Her black veil seemed to cover her bent shoulders, heavy from the year of preparing us for this major event in our lives. What was left? A good confession and a white dress!

But then it happened. The details are blurred now but one picture emerges from those many years ago. It was First Communion Sunday and I, dressed in my Sunday clothes, played alone in our back yard. My dress was blue, not white. I would not be a part of the May procession into the Church. I would not be sitting in seats reserved for children who would receive the Lord for the first time. My child eyes were cast down now and my child pride was humbled.

Years later, as I would share a Saturday breakfast with Sr. Mary Irma, my Grey Nun sister, she liked to tease, "Tell me again how you flunked First Communion." She would chuckle, unbelievingly, as I retold the episode. It became a popular story to retell on casual Saturdays. But to spice up a rather straight story, I added a punch line. "My mom and dad were so embarrassed by having their daughter fail that we soon moved out of the neighborhood." Yes, we moved that August. But, the real reason? Twins! Our growing family needed a larger home.

Oh, I did make my First Communion. It was in our new church. The line of second graders moved piously toward the altar and two fifth graders closed the line.

For everything there is a season... What is the right time, a proper chronology for particular experiences to take place in life? We are born, some in nine months, some prematurely or others induced. We die, as children, as adults, in old age. We are marshaled through school by age, yet some are younger or older than the grade standard. It was my fifth grade First Communion that makes me take note of "off time" experiences.

We hear that Jesus came in the fullness of time. That time began with what we call the Christmas season, his time of birth. He was born a Jew and scripture attests to his timely experiences- he was circumcised after eight days. According to the Law of Moses: "Every male that opened the womb shall be consecrated to the Lord" so Mary presented him for consecration. It was in that season that prophetic words pronounced by Simeon and Anna recognized the vocation of the child Jesus- savior of all including the gentiles, calling him Redeemer. Later at twelve, was Jesus aware of this vocation as he spoke with the teachers in the Temple? Then back home, Jesus waited until at age thirty he would emerge, enter into the prophetic time.

Is God concerned with our sense of right time or does God use time to accomplish his will? What is the insight or grace that touched the heart of a ten year old? Was this the moment when the desire for Christ was burned into a disappointed heart, when the seed of vocation was buried there?

MISTAKEN IDENTITY

Angel Unaware.....
The dress was light blue, long, with lines of lace at the waist and hem. Two white wings helped to define who I was as I began my walk to school. A green, button down coat sheltered this angel from the crisp, biting October day. Clearly this was an angel. No, not an angel from heaven but an angel in the persona of a third grader- or more accurately, a third grader on her way to the class Halloween party.

As I walked the familiar path to PS #42, other children joined the daily route. One angel walked among them. Strange that none looked like the traditional ghosts or goblins or the many other Halloween favorites. Weren't other classes celebrating the holiday today? Our third grade must be special, I mused, as angel steps moved me from my locker to our classroom. This would certainly be a fun day!

Fun day indeed! The teacher approached the angel hoping to hear the truth that the angel had appeared on the wrong day. That confession, that admission, however, was not forthcoming. Out of the mouth of this angel were denial and the certainty that today was the proclaimed holiday. After all who should know better than an angel?... or a third grader?

A fallen angel left school that day, no choirs to accompany her, unaware of grown up days ahead, and real angels that would accompany her.

Unaware of Angels.....
Rome, four decades after, and three thousand miles away from, PS#42, welcomed a former angel, now in her golden years. I walked among pilgrims wearing the blue scarves that marked us as friends of Marguerite d'Youville- newly proclaimed Saint.

The days before the canonization were spent sight seeing. Rome unveiled its history and culture before us- its ruins and churches, its catacombs and Vatican treasures, its river, its people, its art and language.

It was on one of those days of exploration that the unexpected happened. My roommate and I were on a bus and lost. Help! Two other passengers and the driver! Would their Italian and my Spanish be a saving communication? The passengers, a young couple wearing white jackets, volunteered, "We speak English." We named our destination and they responded, "Follow us." And that is what we did, followed them. They kept strangely silent, walking ahead of us until we reached a bus stop. After pointing us to the correct bus they left, white jackets fading into....? seeming to disappear into... ?

We didn't raise any questions about the young couple wearing the white jackets- that led us and then left us- until later when we were recalling the events of the day. There seemed to be only one answer. Only then did we become aware of who they might be who walked with us, who pointed the way, on this special Roman holiday.

I suppose my real identity was clear to those who watched me trek along disguised as an angel. Not only did they know the truth- I was not an angel, but they knew something I didn't, that this was not Halloween.

Scripture is filled with angelic figures who appear to point people in a direction that will lead them toward some good. I think of Lot in the Old Testament and Joseph and Mary of Magdela in the New Testament.

Lot had an encounter with two angels at Sodom. He was offering hospitality to whom he simply believed to be guests. This meeting later revealed the identity of the guests- messengers from God, angels, who were to lead Lot and his family out of Sodom and point them to safety, to the "hills" and to a small town nearby. These two strangers later revealed themselves as angelic messengers.

For Joseph, his encounter with angels came in dreams. "Do not be afraid to take Mary as your wife...Get up and take the child and his mother with you, and escape into Egypt..." How do I respond to my dreams? Do dreams have anything to do with the choices I make?

I think of Mary of Magdela who came to anoint Jesus. At the tomb she was first greeted by two angels in white sitting where the body of Jesus had been. They spoke as if to ask her need, "Why are you weeping?" Once the two figures heard her plea, the answer came, but from another.

Mary turned to whom she supposed to be the gardener. It seems that what she sought from the angels in white led her to hear the voice of Jesus pointing her to carry his message to the disciples.

When I look back at that experience in Rome, I see what I had not seen clearly at the time. I have become aware that God's messengers appear in our need. I am aware that like the angel that was really just a little girl, there are some grown ups who are really angels. I am aware that I should not neglect that reality by making a thoughtless mistaken identity.

But in Rome where the very history and culture emit the spirit of religion how could I be unaware of the angelic presence that I experienced?

A KID ON STAGE

My classmates called me forth. Even before I could claim any oratorical charism, they urged me: "Join the speaking contest. You'll be good!" Thus began an interesting journey that would forge a trail from a first trial and failure to another trial and...

The essay I chose was, "The House with the Golden Windows." My prompter was Marilyn, a favorite and intelligent classmate. Her task: whisper the next word or phrase should I forget. The rule was that Mr. B, our teacher, would stand up to signal that a speaker had a minute left to complete her presentation.

As I stood before the school assembly, the words of the essay flowed from the mouth of the young teen who was favored to win this contest. Then the unspeakable happened. I stopped. No words followed. Marilyn, totally engrossed in listening, failed to follow the text. I was alone. In sympathy for the speechless orator, Mr. B. stood up before the appointed time allowing me to leave the stage.

Yes, I left that stage. But a new challenge became a stage for me. I recognized that the embarrassment of that event was less a concern than the fear of public speaking itself. What could I do? High School provided oratorical opportunities. There was the debate class where we practiced the art of argumentation and the drama course with an emphasis on developing one's interpretive and expressive skills. Each was a valuable moment on my stage and I enjoyed walking across it in the security of four walls and twenty five companions. .Each class reached into a part of me, embraced and nurtured gifts yet unexpressed. Still that unspoken fear lingered.

Oh no! Spoken words stirred up the memory of words unspoken on a stage four years earlier: "our drama class of seniors will be putting on a Christmas play"... in public!. During the school assembly!" As the teacher assigned the parts, my downcast eyes and tightened body were rejecting the possibility of my being chosen. I breathed in relief as the last person was selected. The next words turned it all topsy-turvy. And, Ruth, you will do a presentation of "Keeping Christmas" by Henry Van

Dyke.

Alone, I would be alone in front of the assembly. No actors to surround me. No classmates at my side. Quick flashes of the past renewed my fear. However, this was the present. There was no Marilyn, no Mr. B. to get me off the stage. Instead, there was Miss Zeh to get me on stage, encouraging me with the wisdom of the ages, "Do the thing you fear and the death of fear is certain." Oh, I trembled as I waited my turn that day. But when I left the stage it was after I spoke the last line: "...and, if you can keep it for a day, why not always?"

Today as then, I remember the piece by Van Dyke but not a word of "The House with the Golden Windows."

Isn't it interesting to look back at some stage of our life and to see it in view of who we are today? A poet once said, "all life is a stage and we are the players."

We are the players... chosen, called by God, called by name even before we experienced the warmth of a mother's womb, the light of birth, or our first steps... onto our personal stage. Chosen, for particular roles, to share particular gifts, so that the play is a success!

Some might label this predestination. I like to believe that God shared a piece of himself- a free will, a will to choose the good. That is what we bring to the stage of our life, that is our most precious gift! As we put on our identity and play our part we do so by interpreting the role, freely, but directed by God's grace. Yet, we sometimes falter.

Peter heard the words, words in our hearing as well: Before the cock crows you will deny me three times". Peter stepped onto a special stage in his life. He heard the Lord call his name, his role: "You are Rock". Yet as he put on this graced identity, and even knowing Whom it was that called him, Peter yielded to fear and failed three times.

Like Peter, there are times when we fall silent, when we fail in our parts. It's then that we need to heed the Prompter's whisper.

CAN ANYTHING GOOD COME OUT OF WOOLWORTHS?

Why was I selling socks? My counter was well kept with the neat rows of socks, of various sizes, colors and brands neatly folded and placed in order. But why was I, newly graduated from high school, selling socks?

I graduated high school with a diploma but unclear goals. A high school teacher, yes that is what I wanted to be. On the other hand, I was a fledgling artist, fascinated with the world of Disney. I rounded out my study by completing both the college entrance requirements and those of the Fine Arts department At graduation, when I was confronted with a choice of diplomas, I chose the Fine Arts not the College Entrance English. Why wouldn't they allow me to have College Entrance Fine Arts? With this question lingering, I applied to Buffalo State Teachers College for Elementary Education but never followed through. Thus it was that I found myself at Woolworth's and began a six year hiatus as a sock seller who advanced to assistant office manager.

My father never understood this move. To complicate things, every conversation that took place between us about careers, ended with his serious advice: "Become a court stenographer". Now I have no idea where this suggestion came from except he assured me the money was good. It was a rather strange counsel since my dad himself wanted to be an artist, but his father, a noted cabinet and doll house maker, discouraged his choice.

The Woolworth years were filled with sales experience, with developing a strong sense of responsibility, with growing up in an environment of distinct personalities and values.

But those years, those experiences were finally disrupted by my friend Joan who called halt. "You must go to college", she urged. Then she introduced me to that place which would become my alma mater, graduate me with a B.A. in Spanish with education, and lead me to a life as a Grey Nun-d'Youville College. There, also, I would meet Sheila who would become a life long friend (that not to be determined by our first encounter).

So it was that those years at Woolworth's were not wasted time but a road taken.

"Two roads diverged in a yellow wood..." Robert Frost suggested in the poem. "And I, I took the road less traveled by. And that has made all the difference for me. The poet laments, "sorry I could not travel both". My dilemma over diplomas, careers, schools. all fade into a distant memory as I look forward, look beyond the last thirty five years, and into the adventure of today and the window of retirement.

Yes the road I took, the time with Woolworth's, was a pause in my days that changed my life. Pauses like this may cause one to see only a part of the road we travel, "to where it bent in the undergrowth". Our Provident God is watching over us, loving and nurturing us where we are. Where we are is good...if only for a time.

We do not always comprehend the hidden years. How do we know Jesus? Scripture says he was with his family and grew in wisdom and stature. We do not know what happened when he took that other path, that period of time unknown to us, the "silent" years.

What we quickly discover after Jesus emerges is that he takes a path that leads him to Jerusalem, to his destiny. We see him sure of himself, sure of what he must do. Perhaps he repeats words spoken earlier: "I must be about my Father's business". Graced now with wisdom and stature, he is ready even when others would wonder, "Can anything good come out of Nazareth?"....or Woolworth's?

Don't we rejoice, when we are overwhelmed with the good gifts that come when we emerge, when we realize they were possible only because we took that "other" path for a while? Now I proclaim, "Yes, something good can come out of Woolworth's"!

FIFTY YEARS LATER

We had just dined using our ten dollar Applebee's Christmas gift certificate. Now, Joan and I sat on the balcony of my apartment looking out at the Niagara River. Memories took hold and stories of the Towpath and swimming in these waters near the lighthouse flowed easily into the present. When the chill of a slight breeze urged us to go inside, the remembered events continued to flow freely.

When did we first meet? Fifty years later, no defining moment could be marked. What drew two late teenagers together? We came from different sides of the Catholic tracks- Joan from 12 years of Catholic schooling and I from being a public. Being public meant I was a Catholic who went to public school. Then there was the unmarked division of the Riverside area where we lived, somewhere around Esser Avenue at All Saints' Church, with Joan on one side and I on the other.

So, as we sat there remembering, it was becoming obvious that we had become good friends and that was our historic reality. We had often recalled a greeting card verse and claimed it as ours chanting its words:

> What made us good friends, you and I
> I think I know the reason why
> The best in you
> And the best in me, hailed each other because they knew
> That ever and ever since life began
> Our being friends was part of God's plan.

Aha! That was the defining moment, one outside of us, one belonging to God, one revealing the together-experiences of two good Catholic gals, one that now measures fifty years.

We continued the random remembering and chuckled over each memory. Yes, and while many were worthy of a laugh, just as many were stepping stones in the miracle of friendship. Many were the movements of God, disguised, perhaps, in simple events but always a grace that came alive when two gathered in his name.

Joan was a daily communicant. Maybe I could do that. Joan was involved in church activities. Maybe I could spend a Friday evening checking pinochle tally cards. Joan used her gift of athletics to coach younger teens. Maybe I could coach a team and even expand into directing CYO plays. Joan was a good bowler, ice skater and a fair skier. Maybe I could join her in those activities even when skating and skiing found me breaking bones rather than records. Joan was always in touch with our priests and willing to assist where needed. Maybe I could join her in doing the background tasks required for a conference retreat.

Joan led me into a world of motley experiences where God was with us and my own spirituality was being enriched even as was her own.

We recalled the Friday evening at the Alcoe Bar and chatting about college over our ice cream sundaes. A decision was coming to fruition. "You must go to college," she urged. Joan was continuing her Catholic education at d'Youville College. Maybe it was time for me to leave Woolworth's and pursue higher education. If Joan could do it, why not me?

Time seemed against me since the semester was just weeks away and I had not taken the entrance exams. Would I even be accepted? For Joan there was no hurdle. In her usual leadership style, the business would be taken on. We hustled to her house where a 7 pm phone call arranged a meeting with the Dean- a meeting in one half hour. Joan's next task was to transform this jeans wearing, Friday night, casually dressed person into an acceptable looking Catholic college candidate interviewee. It was simple. The jeans must be rolled to the knees and then all of me was cloaked in Joan's trench coat. The interview, my first experience with a Grey Nun, would be successful despite the hidden me.

The end? No! Joan had brought me in touch with a superficial reality-getting a college education. But who can pre-guess all outcomes? Who would know that the two sundae eating friends at the ice cream bar were living a grace moment? Who would know that the silent stirring of a vocation, a once sixth grader's desire to do mission work, would begin to find life outside of an unspoken dream? It took the mystery of grace- Joan, me, and a Grey Nun. But that night, two friends went home, unaware of acting in grace, and laughed about the day's events.

God was always more than in the heart of my friend. Joan's activities and her choices   always reflected the faith that was so precious to her. I have been privileged to walk with her these fifty years. The hinge in our relationship has always remained our God, our faith...and just enjoying each other's company.

Remember John, the beloved apostle? An interesting difference between his Good News and that of Matthew, Mark and Luke is that he never mentions his defining moment of meeting Jesus. Rather, John writes the end of the story in the later years of his life.. He reveals the underlying truth that Jesus was God. I resonate with this as an analogy of the Joan-Ruth story. Our experiences are measured, not by recounting the events of fifty years, but that at this writing the underlying truth of our stories is Joan and Ruth are good friends.

Apostles, Jesus chose twelve to walk with him. Then he empowered Peter, gave him a role that would cross over two millennia. At this point in the long history of Apostles we name John Paul II. The Church story is living its reality today. Can you list all those others who have held the keys which were charged to Peter's care? But we do know the end to date is John Paul II.

I boldly paraphrase John's last words in his Gospel:

> This Ruthy is the one who vouches for these things
> about our friendship
> and has written them down.
> There were many other experienced events
> that Joan and Ruth shared; if all were written down,
> this book itself, I suppose, would not hold
> all the pages that would have to be written
> (To Joan, Christmas 2004)

WHEN ONE DOOR CLOSES...

"You'll have to leave; I've reserved this room"! Was it the voice or the tone? She won the disagreement about who was entitled to use the room. As the door closed behind me, I was unaware of a door yet to be opened, opened to a friendship of forty years and counting.

Sheila entered my life, my door, on a sour note. Sheila, the classmate who appeared in my sophomore year! The one thing we shared was membership in our college class of '62. That sour note would soon be sweetened by a person in the middle, Joan. On the one hand, Joan knew Sheila and had become her friend. On the other, Joan and I had already shared years of friendship. Like a magnet, we were mystically drawn together by the relationship we each had with Joan and a new door opened. Looking back, I call it Divine Providence.

And so another door had opened, the door to the Sheila-Ruth friendship. Friendship, a beautiful treasure! Like any treasure, one might have to wipe away what hides its beauty- even a first meeting covered by disagreement. Only then is something special revealed. In an unremembered event or time, Sheila became this special treasure for me.

What makes friends? God's Providence and our response to his hints! So it was with us who invited that grace in spite of our bad beginning. Friends- those who become for each other, because of each other, a source of God's grace to each other, leading each other into their growth in wisdom and grace! We are friends who share a joy in life, who share play and poetry, debating differences, recognizing strengths, and ultimately facing diminishment, change and an uncertain future.

Our friendship, Sheila's and mine (and indeed that middle person, Joan) reflects all of this.

I look back on the Sheila I know, one first named Noel who would discover a door that closed on her and a new one that she entered when she was three years old. That open door offered Sheila a family and expressions of mutual love.

Doors began to open, close and then new doors opened, and so did a familiar cycle. There was the door of the convent that soon closed. And when she stepped into another door, now the teacher-Sheila brought with her a creative personality and religious spirit. Once more, Sheila was called to experience another door closed, this one by illness. But, there was yet another door, a door she took on with a familiar vigor, despite a still more declining health.

Today, I see in Sheila the strength and courage of a woman in diminishment. Her body attacked by illness does not yield to that physical trauma but rises in her smile, her wit, her scratchy voice, as she continues to enjoy a still higher relationship with her God- tasting of his goodness, praising his works and loving and witnessing to his children and living the life offered her. Yes, all these are the emergence of a soul that I first met as sour when a door was closed on me. Now, I admit and pray that the life relationship and lessons of this friend may be etched on my soul- of her friend who first walked with her through that other door which opened.

When one door closes another opens! Wasn't this the experience of those early followers of Jesus, men and women? It was certainly true of the Twelve who, at his call, left behind a life and people to follow Jesus into an uncertain future. There were Judas and Peter, one who entered a relationship but finally refused the open door and the other who entered and endured as he stumbled through a new friendship. We might look on those who were healed by Jesus: the blind man who left a life of blindness and entered a world of light…the woman spared by the stones of condemnation and invited into a new way of living…the son eager to depart who would return to the loving, celebrating, embrace of his father.

And, what of Jesus himself? God-man, carpenter's son, virgin's gift… His doors? The door of birth in a stable: the entrance of the cave and resurrection from death; the carpenter's place and carving of wooden pieces: the grasslands and inviting belief; the child leaving his parents troubled: the meeting leaving religious leaders informed and wondering; the closed door of the Temple of worship: the lifted up wooden cross and his final prayer to God. Old doors closed, new doors opened!

Doors, doors, doors...

I reflect on friendship and all that happens when I allow one door to close and I enter the one that opens to me. So it has been with Sheila.

———————

2 January 2008. Sheila has gone through her last door. May God and his angels greet her at the heavenly door.

WANNABES

I think Beth and I had a destiny to meet...Providence knew that there was something about the two of us that would make friendship work. God sure worked in crooked lines to create that relationship.

"Wannabes". That was who we were on a Christmas eve night. It was our first meeting, at the d'Youville College front door. We each had received an invitation to attend the midnight Mass and were waiting for the hostess- Beth for her friend Betty and I for my former postulant mistress. Everything soon came together when the one person we each knew by other names appeared.

We were happy about the invitation, the Mass, and later Beth and I sat down to talk a bit. Our conversation revealed us as "wannabes". Beth had entered the convent some years earlier and then made a very unconventional departure. I was entering the third year of novitiate when illness at home brought me to make a hard decision to leave. Now as we talked, it was obvious that we had a common desire- to renter the convent, the Grey Nuns.

So it was that I met my dear friend, Bethy. Not long after that meeting, God paved the way for the "wannabes" to have their common wish, to don the Grey Nun habit once more!

Beth was no ordinary nun. Oh, she was a woman of faith; she was a woman committed to a catechetical ministry, faithful to the charism of the Grey Nuns; she was a woman much respected because of her extraordinary openness and kindness to all who shared or needed her ministry or friendship. But, ordinary? No indeed! The question might be posed, "a nun or a woman?" The answer provides the resolution- she's just being Bethy. And many who came to know her and love her, called her Bethy.

What would mark our friendship? She often reminded me that actually I was her #3 friend. You know, I never minded my position on her friend list because I knew that when Bethy wanted time with me I was content to be #3 or so, wannabe- ready to be available. Being Bethy, those times were as unconventional as everything else that could describe her.

When you were with Bethy you were with her truth. There was no pretense. She allowed herself a freedom from worrying about what others might think about her or her actions.

Bethy walked a hard physical journey carrying the burden of Lupus. I held her hand and shared her tears when her doctor announced the advanced condition that would require dialysis. I wonder if her fear was relieved by his words, "Oh you'll die like anyone else, some day but not from this." I was with Bethy years before in a Paoli hospital when she shared the dread of her recently diagnosed disease, when she read about it's devastation to the body. A nurse scolded her for playing detective (a Bethy action) at the nurse's station and assured her that the medical book she took was outdated.

She was a hard worker at a ministry that often demanded her evenings or weekends. Yet she enjoyed life beyond ministry. Bethy was playful. She loved board games, word games, cards and yes, even a bit of gambling. She knew that #3 or so was at her beck and call even, though reluctantly, to breaking rules for the sake of a game...rather, I confess, to play with my friend. So it was that when hospitalized (and that was frequently) Bethy invited me not to come during evening visiting hours. That was reserved for other people. I was to appear after 8:30 pm- post visiting hours- and bring along a game. I came, but unlike my friend, I was prone to look over my shoulder, fearful of being caught.

When she was tired, your couch might be her place of respite, her place of comfort. I think back to her visit with me at St. Leo's in New York City. Her arrival was unexpected. I opened the door to a very sick Bethy. Despite that we had a fine visit, Bethy stretched out on my bed and I, sitting nearby, just enjoying each other and sharing our stories.

I am grateful for the twenty five years of "wannabe" experiences with Bethy. Even being #3 provided me so many intimate, serious and playful moments with my friend. Those moments reached through years and Grey Nun places- from Buffalo to Yardley to Melrose to Paoli to Corona and back to Buffalo.

Bethy made another trip to the Motherhouse at Yardley but yearned to return to Buffalo. I wonder if she was reflecting on a thought that she tried to keep way back in her mind- " everyone in my family dies young". Despite many concerns that she remain at the Motherhouse, Bethy asked me to bring her home. I think of the poet who called home "the place where, when you have to go there, they have to take you in". I reflect now on what those words meant to my friend Bethy. Hers was a sad homecoming and I was looking over my shoulder once more. No matter, my "wannabe friend" asked this of me and I would not refuse.

Bethy died peacefully doing one of her favorite things, watching a Bills football game. Rest in peace, Bethy, you completed the many yards of life and now you are experiencing the joy of a final touchdown.

I was a wannabe in Bethy's life- a wannabe her friend. Memories of her are renewed as I often drive by her home, where "they had to take her in".

"Allow us to sit one at your right hand and one at your left..."

Recall the brothers, James and John, who approached Jesus to ask a favor. Those wannabe fellows were chosen by Jesus to be among the twelve he had called, called to share his brief ministry. They were doing that when the question arose about being first. They even affirmed that they were wiling to share the bitter part: "We can" is their response to Jesus' offer to drink the cup that He would drink. Even so, Jesus kept them among the twelve...yet still wannabes. When Jesus called the disciples James was #3 and his brother John #4. I draw a personal parallel here. Note too, that Scripture names who Jesus' best friend was. It is the one called beloved, John. Not even Andrew or Peter who were the first two called to walk with Him.

So it is as we drink our cups and share our lives with the various people we meet. Being first on a friendship list is relative. I think we walk in the seasons of relationship where numbers count less than the gift of friendship itself, where it is how much of another's cup we are willing to drink rather than who is served first.

I was a wannabe friend. Yet, being #3 or so, never deprived me of sharing a part of Beth's life and her cup.

MONTAGE- FRIENDS, ANGELS, KINGS AND YELLOW ROSES

Friendship has many faces. My friends' faces reflect heritages distinguished by and inclusive of color, nationality, and religion. I call them friends, yet I meet each in a different place with a distinct reason for the name friend. Each becomes a unique montage

One among them is Mary. It happens that Mary is a New England Italian. I think her close relationship with her family members and her pride in all aspects of their lives speaks of that heritage. I also think that is why Mary was able to become a friend to many and different people. She cared about their lives and expressed that care freely. They frequently responded with a gift of yellow roses, Mary's favorite.

I arrived at my new assignment with a broken leg. So it was that I met Mary, herself disabled by chronic foot problems. There was no hesitation in reaching out a hand of care to another's need. Perhaps it was this Mary, doing my laundry that opened a door of friendship. Laundry, one's personal items cared for by another! Friends, people who could begin to share personal stories! Friends, people who care! Friends, those who reach out despite their own infirmity!

Mary and I shared experiences beyond laundry. She was a fellow traveler, my guide, as I learned my way around New York City. A non driver is sometimes a better guide. I was a welcome visitor to her ministry to the deaf and her visits to those in nursing homes. Pictures introduced me to her family and personal visits to meet them assured me of their importance to her life and her sharing both with me. Later, on another turf, I could share meetings with my family. When I was busy producing student plays, Mary was not far behind being present just for support. And games! They are a way of losing time together. We were like kids as we laughed through "Password" because of Mary's New England accent, when "guard" became "God". How brave of her, pianist par excelance, to try to teach this tone deaf ear how to play and to subject everyone to the simple strains of Ode to Joy...over and over and...The end of my music career.

Do you believe that we met an angel? Yes, an Angel! It happened as we were on the way to an August retreat. En route, I suggested we pull off the road to a scenic view of the Hudson River. The parking area was empty, likely due to the heavy clouds threatening a downpour. Because of the extreme heat and the need to keep the car cool, I left the car running and the AC on. Immediately on closing the door, I realized it had locked. So much for scenic views. Now, our view was on an empty, off the highway, parking area, a sky lit by sheets of lightning and the sounding claps of thunder. We sat on a rock pondering and praying about our situation. Our prayer preceded any rain and produced a van entering the area. The obliging driver was willing to take my AAA number and promised to call them in our behalf. The two children with her were unusually silent, disinterested in our discussion. When I suggested that she might want to view the site before leaving, her response: "I had no intention of stopping here." No intention? Mary and I sat down again. Once more we pondered what happened and believed our prayer brought us an angel. And, the angel brought us the help that would open the door.

When I returned from a home Christmas vacation, I was telling about my mom's lost contact lens and how I came to find it. I recalled the details: searching all over, afraid to vacuum the rug and losing the lens forever. My recourse was Scripture. Trusting that God would lead me to a word that would direct me to the lens, I opened the bible at random. The page fell open to Kings. Well, I'll try again. Again, Kings and war stories! God, what could this have to do with the lost lens? I will give you another chance. Just tell me if I will find it. The words leaped from the random page: "Of course I want to". The next morning while serving breakfast…, Here, Mary interrupted to reveal what a good Italian would know: "You found the lens on or near a cake". Yes, the cake, King's cake, was on the table near where I set down the plate of food and the lens rested on top. Sorry for not trusting you, God.

Retirement! Sometimes it takes one's breath away. One's world changes, one's days change. Sometimes one's needs grow. I suspect retirement is not Mary's favorite thing "to do". I think it is time to perk her up when we visit next. Yellow roses are in order.

Picture another montage. A stable: a Jewish family with a new born son; a star; choirs of hovering angels; shepherds pausing near; kings arriving. How often we have looked upon the scene, a memory of two thousand years ago!

In the living montage, for this Jewish family, it was necessary to make the journey to identify themselves for the census. Their stop at this stable, this time of birth, was comforted by shepherd- friends who surrounded them. They were the first to respond to a star that would lead them to this place, to this moment of intimate sharing. The new born babe would enjoy his first sounds- angels singing, with those first visitors. Finally, the montage presents Kings with their gifts- gold, frankincense and myrrh.

How like our own montages is this lived event. We can look into it each Christmas and perhaps, each time, glimpse our own experiences. Scripture offers us other montages for other seasons. They call us to enter them reflectively and there resume moments of graced friendship with our Lord. Perhaps, in response to his ultimate gift, we might pray "thank you" ... and place a yellow rose at the foot of the cross.

A NO-GLITZ MINISTRY:
Words from a Chaplain School Buddy

(1) The Email to Ruth

I never expected this email or the words it bore. As the words rose from
the screen, they reached me in some vulnerable spirit place that brings a
sudden rush of tears. I began

> *Ruth:*
> *I sent this nomination to CCMA and wanted to share it with you.*
> *I suspect the 'powers that be' will keep with tradition and go for glitz*
> *in making this award to someone who has budgets and support for*
> *"kick-ass" programs. If they really grasped community college*
> *campus ministry, our national organization and our conventions*
> *would be a bit different , eh? Thank you for being a sister in the ministry*
> *who shares in and understands the vital work that we do ministering*
> *not necessarily to the Body of Christ, but really loving all the people of*
> *God!*
>
> *Blessings! Jane*

(2) The Nomination to the CCMA

> *November 20th, 2002 Greetings!*
>
> *Thirty years ago, I sat in the Newman Center at Miami University with*
> *Charlie Forsyth. Touched by the war stories of this 'one-legged wonder,'*
> *I was even more touched by his deep faith and courage. I will never*
> *forget his understanding that ministry is service "where the people are"*
> *not always where the church is. "Get over on campus", he told us.*
> *"That's where your ministry is." Ruth has known and lived this in*
> *so many ways.*
>
> *Courage does not always roar. Sometimes it is the quiet voice*
> *at the end of the day saying, "I will try again tomorrow."*
> *(M Radmacher)*
>
> *I know well this kind of ministry on a community college campus and I*
> *know that Ruth is a woman of deep faith and courage who continues,*

in very ordinary ways, to make faith and hope and love with the ordinary people and things around her. For this I honor her and her ministry.

Awarding the Forsyth award to Ruth Penksa is an award to all the 'ordinary' campus ministers who have no "knock-your-socks-off programs, or chair regional or national events, or perhaps even have budgets to afford national conventions but who faithfully get up every morning and love the campus all over again.

I ask you to consider this focus and Sister Ruth for this year's Forsyth award.

Sincerely, Jane Steinhauser

(3) Response to Jane
Overwhelmed by this nomination and understanding the no-glitz clause included, I responded to Jane:

Dear Jane,

I am absolutely overwhelmed by your thoughts. Right now your comments bring tears to my eyes. I will hold your words as a precious gift from you to me. No matter the award...I thank you. What I will do, is to copy your comments and make my own private plaque (hope that isn't vain).

Hey Doc, you sure did dig around to think about this ol' nun... in the sunset (I hope) of all those years. But we nuns keep on goin'. Retirement??? What's that...hahaha. I have been lucky to enjoy my ministry here despite lots of hits from the administration (tales to share another time).

Cheerfully,
Your companion on the journey of campus ministry and faith...Ruth

---

Yes, "glitz" will win the Forsythe Award. That is not to say that the nominee is undeserving of recognition. Winners have already displayed the wonderful works of their ministry and their service to the mission of the Catholic Campus Ministers National Association.

What of me? My name submitted in nomination reminded me of the mother of Zebedee's sons. She came to Jesus to put them in nomination for two glory spots, spots for two sons already selected by Jesus to be disciples- a place on Jesus' right and one on his left. Well, for Jesus, it was not to be a matter of seating but a matter of "drinking [my] cup", that if you would be first, you must be servant to others.

I think Jane was suggesting that I have been sipping from that cup- "that ministry is service 'where the people are' not always where the church is"- visible in some glorious spot. I have been content to accept a discipleship of service. The two sons, disciples, were quick to say "we can" when prompted by Jesus, "Can you drink the cup that I will drink?"

Jane has eloquently described ministry at a community college. And, she speaks from her own years of experience there.

I question, where have twenty years gone? What has happened in that span of time? What happened over the years was not a "seat"- some prominent place offered me. Rather, this daughter-disciple of Jesus was moved about indiscriminately without concern for a ministry of presence. Five moves, reminded me that Jesus had nowhere to lay his head, no church of welcome, but always places where the people were. The fifth move settled ministry next to the place where it all began twenty years ago.

Jesus did not promise a seat on his right or his left. Jane's "no-glitz ministry" echoes Jesus' insistence that if you would be first among the disciples you must be their servant.

I did not receive the award.

ANOTHER DOOR...

I looked out at a motley audience as I began. You have heard about Sheila's fidelity to the Church she loved and to its members, the body, even when her own body was suffering diminishment. You heard and perhaps you have experienced this sign.

You have heard about her many achievements in her short life. You have heard and perhaps you have experienced this sign.

There was another sign... It was Little Christmas 1942...a baby was born and a mother called her Noel. Here, no joyous proclamations, the only strains a mother's voice, perhaps sadly giving up the child. Here no father to offer a promise of protection. Did visitors come to see baby Noel or friends shower her with gifts? Soon, she was alone, waiting for that someone who would embrace her, give her a new name and welcome her into a new family.

How unlike the scene where a babe was birthed on the first Christmas! We imagine the choirs of angelic greeters, of shepherds hovering near. A mother embraces the baby and a father stands present to both. Visitors come bearing gifts. It is a holy night, it is a holy family.

But that Christmas season blessed her with a new name Sheila. She became the familiar, active, involved, intelligent, spontaneous, fun personality, a bit bossy one too. These signaled the person that broke into my life when we met in college. The memories I share reflect signs of the Sheila I came to know.

Intelligent! Oh yes, Sheila was that. But there was Miss Planas and Spanish class. My friend was a history major and hardly adept at language. When Sheil asked me, a Spanish major, to help her study for her exam, I offered her my study preparation papers. She should do fine at memorizing, a skill surpassing mine. A phone call proclaimed her grade- a D. In broken English Miss Planas questioned: "Señorita, why did you write an essay about a book we did not study in your class?" Different books in different classes, Sheila had absorbed the information from my class work.

But, there are second chances and third ones too. We were new teachers who had recently been in a car accident. She sued me and I sued the car at fault. No matter, there was money for two to travel- destination South America.

We arrived in Peru and Sheila was anxious to meet our host family. I offered her the greeting for I am happy to meet you- mucho gusto en conocerle. However, I suggested she use the common shorter form- mucho gusto. Not Sheil. She would assert with boldness: "mucho gusto en comerle". Translation: I am happy to "eat" you!

After a month, we prepared to leave and the D student of Spanish tried again. When mamá, who spoke no English, asked when we would make a return visit, my friend blurted out: "en tres anos" (a body part) instead of en tres años (years).

New teacher syndrome! Were these incidents typical of all new to the profession? We found our shared first year of teaching a highly explosive experience. We arrived late a few times…well maybe many! So, at their beckoning, we agreed to portray our tardiness in a two person skit in the parents' annual pageant. Although Sheil was a gifted actress, the performance was not appreciated by the Assistant Principal Nun. No "Trends of Teaching" class ever warned us "don't teach while perched on your teacher desk" or "be sure to send in lesson plans if you are absent". Being friends left me to accept Sheila's reprimands. Yes, Sister Mary Lurking of the Holy Spirit was not oblivious to these and our other failings. But we became aware of her disapprovals. Yet, in her classroom domain and in other settings, Sheila was a beloved, intelligent, history teacher, producer of plays, and often a minister of comfort to her students. And, I think she gave up tardiness.

Bring in the clowns! Sheil was dramatic, a schooled actress. She was also a devoted comic, and often made fun of herself. As her illness pecked away at her physical beauty, she would smile broadly and proclaim: "I look like Barry Fitzgerald". Sadly, she did. Sheil loved Marcel Marceau and mime. Mime would serve her when, later, she would suffer with throat cancer. A gift of a clown doll always won a happy thanks and then, when words were not formed freely, a nod or broad smile of appreciation or a hug. She reached out to the last clown I offered her and affectionately lifted the doll from his wicker chair for a brief look and an embrace. Sheila, my clown friend, in her final days, was living the silence of a mime, unable to speak, signaling what was her greeting or her need.

At one point in our friendship, Sheil had taken a step that would separate us, just for a brief time. An email suggests what the step was and the outcome.

> "I am so sorry to hear about Sheila. I remember her so fondly from the novitiate. She was trying to quit smoking at the time, so she had a pass for gum and candy... which she shared with us non-smokers, as I recall"

Aha, sounds like my Sheila.

Robert Frost wrote: Home is the place where when you have to go there they have to take you in. I welcomed her return and took her into close friendship once more.

What makes friends? Gods Providence and our response to His hints, his signs! So it was with us who invited that grace. We were friends who shared playful moments, poetry, debating differences, recognizing strengths and ultimately facing diminishment, change and the uncertainty of the future.

As I spoke, I was aware that now certainty surrounded us. My friend Sheil, one first named Noel, had taken another step in the story of life. She had gone without me.

We shared the heights of Machu Pichu, in Peru, where we might touch heaven and we shared our last visits listening to non-rhythmic sounds of life sustaining machines, praying, holding hands. Sheila has left me and she has reached out to touch heaven alone.

God bless you my friend. Happy Birthday, see ya later.
...the life of Sheila, 6 January 1940 – 2 January 2006

Scripture introduces us to figures that are silenced- sight, voice, life surrendered to God's will. What significance does each one's loss have with my friend's whose loss would not be restored? Paul, a soldier loses his sight; Zechariah, a priest, his speech; Lazarus, friend of Jesus, dies.

Jesus does something interesting by having each suffer a loss in order to offer a sign. Paul's vision of the Christ results in three days of blindness. His lost sight restored, Paul will be what he was not before on the stage of his life – a strong, authoritative, military man, a sign of Roman power. He will emerge as a sign of faith, ready to proclaim the Word even to his own death.

A doubting Zechariah loses his voice when he cannot believe his aging wife would conceive a child. "You will be silenced and have no power of speech until this is fulfilled". This angelic imposition is released when Elizabeth bears a son and Zechariah names him, John. Zechariah now speaks a prophesy, one assigned to convey God's truth about this son. Zechariah becomes the one who will fill people with awe, holding in their heart all that happened and was spoken in readiness for the still to be revealed John, the Baptizer.

Lazarus died and lay in the tomb for four days. His family and friends testify to his final experience and mourn the life taken from them. A deliberate Jesus does not arrive in time to spare his life. Why not? A sign, perhaps to reveal Himself as son of God, perhaps a reminder of who it is that raises one from death. Perhaps this first resurrection marks the nature of the final resurrection with the assurance that new life will follow.

Sheila's physical diminishment, the physical losses she suffered over many years was the enduring sign of her faith. Unlike the Scriptural figures, there was no turning back, no restoration. Why not? At every moment of loss, Sheila was a sign, letting us know that she loved God no less, reminding us of what love may require.

At first, her "I love God" was spoken, then whispered, then formed in silence on her lips. I suspect that as she entered her final sleep, God was whispering a lullaby: "I love you too, Sheila".

Another door welcomed Sheila.

IN THE GARDEN CALLED EDEN

Eden, a "garden" in the southern tier whose lush earth offers a rich bed where farmers lay their seeds! Eden, the place where Grey Nuns planted the seeds of education for area children! And, as each of those seeds grew, they yielded their gifts- food and people. Both made their way from the garden to awaiting communities.

I came to that place, not to farm, but to assist in planting the seeds of education. I came to be principal in the small Catholic School there. I came to be part of a line of Grey Nuns who had opened that school, who had served there for many years.

Why had I come? The apparent reason was the need for a sister to take on the leadership of the school. The call of Vatican II and a declining number of sisters left few interested or available for the position. Looking back, I know the deeper reason was for me to know Nat. I believe that God planted me there to grow, not as the best principal ever, but to be nurtured, to be loved, to share a relationship that was whole and holy.

Our friendship happened without my really looking. Nat became what I affectionately called "my boss". Because of my particular academic background and gifts, I volunteered to work with the Confirmation program which Nat coordinated. Later, when there was a need, Nat applied to be my secretary at the school.

Who was this woman named Nat, this woman who would be such a blessing in my life? Wife, mother of five, beloved by so many in this community! A convert to Catholicism, she was an inspiration of faith. This was the woman with whom I would have the privilege of spending so many precious hours and experiences in this place that was so much like that other Eden.

We worked well together. We played and prayed together. We talked- on the phone, in the comfort of her home, daily and for many hours. Nat knew how to be a faithful, supportive friend- my faithful and supportive friend. God gave us this special time together.

In this garden, weeds invaded every patch of good intent, attempted to choke every good effort. In the midst of the reality of what was happening, of a spiritual struggle emerging as I tried to endure it all, Nat reached out once more. Cursillo. Nat introduced me to the idea. More, she had arranged my participation. I was enlivened by the experience and when the time was right, I was able to finally leave the garden, unscathed by the choking weeds. There was a reason for coming and a season to look toward.

I left that place, that Eden. My job was done, my life enriched. Oh, I did return a few years later when I was invited to be spiritual director for the new Confirmation program. But I know that the true gift came to me, a gift given in those first days, one that would bloom for a season.

Nat died as she had lived, trusting God. Nat- faithful wife, loving mother, minister to so many children of the garden, servant of the Church, dear friend of the community... Nat, my dear friend!

Indeed, not unlike that other Eden, the beauty and richness that was there, was also a place where something might go wrong. But a love emerged there; an encounter with God was realized there. Would I take back a season of friendship and faith that I knew there? I think not.

When I think of how Jesus made his way to Jerusalem despite a destiny intended to choke his word, his very self, I realize that God leads us forward, enticed by grace, to become who we must be. We need to know that we are not alone. Accompanied by those whom he would call "friends", Jesus would spend time with them, would break bread, offer himself for his friends, for all of us.

Nat and I spent time together and often came together to the Lord's Table. We received the Lord himself and in the talking of the bread we became who we must be, his body- here and visible. Any pain that intruded that mystery would be borne in the spirit of Jesus whose utterance, "Father forgive them", would be the expression of faith, would be the lasting gift that I might leave in the garden. That is the gift I gave Eden for its gift to me of Nat.

I CALLED HER "FRIEND"

I never called her Madre. Nor did I call her by the name tossed around by my college mates, with some affection I am sure- "Chrissey Mae". But the day came when I would call her my friend.

I first met Marie Christine when I appeared in her office that August evening of 1958. A late decision to come to d'Youville, an impromptu phone call made by a friend, brought me face to face with the woman who would be an important part of my life.

Thus the friendship journey of forty four years began, would grow from that first meeting, move into her Spanish class and extend into moments of correction and laughter, from stiff social meetings to times of personal sharing. It grew from the woman who was Dean, who was Spanish professor, who was Sister into the one who would be my mentor, my teacher, my friend.

I stood in a kind of awe in her Spanish class where perfection was expected. Fear was the motivation in my becoming a good Spanish student but appreciation finally led me to choose Spanish as my major. Marie Christine had won on both counts.

Marie Christine, Sister Marie Christine. I watched this woman. I noticed her mended domino. I saw her respond to the bell calling her to prayer leaving me with a quick "see you later." My awareness of her Grey Nunness began to mix with a passion for service- born in a once sixth grader, now a college student. Could I possibly stand with the woman as her Grey Nun Sister?

How patiently she waited for me to form the words that I found hard top say: "I would like to be a Grey Nun." Her assuring response was followed by a sense of welcome. Later, I would shed tears as I told her I had not been accepted. "Is God calling you to become a nun or a Grey Nun?!", she challenged. As I pondered the question and was pursuing other possibilities, her phone call to me assured me she wasn't giving up on my becoming a Grey Nun. Sometimes Marie Christine moved in rather subtle ways to make things happen. This was one such time. She would tell me in secret, never to tell how I knew, that Mother Jane

Frances would be in the area, that I should make an appointment to see her. She told me what I must be sure to say to Mother. I think that Marie Christine had done some homework and was leading me to my vocation as a Grey Nun.

Our friendship endured the years. The time we shared was broken by the call of our ministries. But, when we did sit down to talk, the strong bond of friendship was renewed, the assurance of mutual love was spoken.

I regret not having time with my friend after her move for appropriate health care, from our Motherhouse to a nearby Health Manor. My hope was to be with her during the next congregational weekend meeting in 2002 at the Motherhouse. I am sorry she did not wait for my visit. Perhaps, as she answered her final bell, she was once more saying "see you later, Ruth."

"If you had been here my brother would not have died." Both Martha and Mary uttered these words of faith. Their expectation was that the presence of Jesus, Lazarus' friend, and the One who had opened the blind man's eyes, would have prevented the death of their brother. Yet, despite his late arrival, Jesus indeed would raise up Lazarus from death! His actions were deliberate- he arrived late on purpose; he raised Lazarus intentionally. This was a defining moment. "Father, I speak for all these who stand around me, so that they may believe it was you who sent me."

Two thousand years after that event, I resonate with the belief of the two women when they respond to Jesus' words: "...if anyone believes in me, even though he dies, he will live, and whoever lives and believes in me will never die."

"Do you believe this?"

Jesus is asking me! "Yes", I hear myself respond as I tearfully think of the one whose own faith echoed that of Martha and Mary's, "Yes Lord, I believe that you are the Christ, the Son of God..."

Marie Christine's life was lived in that belief. She had chosen to bear the religious name that defined that trust, "Christine." As I reflect on that "yes" and on the vibrant life of this Christ-follower, I know that my moments with this Sister of mine are not lost in some gloomy grave but are lifted up where we will share the glory of God, where I will recognize the woman I called friend.

IT MUST BE SATURDAY

As I walked down the steps of City Campus, I was aware of taking my last steps after twenty five years as Campus Minister and I reflected on my first walk up those steps.

It was the summer of '82. I entered the massive Gothic structure covering an entire city block. Dubbed the old post office, it was recently adapted for use as a college. I was greeted by the great sky lighted atrium that dominated the central portion of the building and was surrounded by four floors of arched galleries and pale ecru walls. As I stood there, I felt an upward surge, an enticement to respond to the scriptural invitation of my prayer. The words echoed in the vastness of what I was witnessing. They began:

> "Yahweh loves his city founded on the holy mountain...
> He has glorious predictions to make of you, city of God!"

This September Saturday, would end much differently from my entry. I walked down the steps alone, unnoticed, no thank you. At our North Campus, another was making a similar departure.

Our joint letter about forced retirement from Campus Ministry was addressed to the college. It began:

> *"As a result of the decision of the Diocesan study "Journey of Faith and Grace", Campus Ministry at Erie Community College will be discontinued..."*
>
> And continued:
>
> *We pause to reflect on the welcome we have received from the College Community, from the thousands of students who have benefited by our presence among them- with our strong commitment to helping them with their educational, physical and spiritual goals...*
>
> *We extend our gratitude to the Administrators/Board of Trustees who first accepted our presence on Campus and for the continued support offered us in all [those] years.*
>
> *We leave with the sense of the history that proudly links us to*

104

ErieCommunityCollege. We leave saddened by this day of our present history with you- by the cost of service to our students and faculty, by setting aside friendships, by leaving an empty space in the halls of our three campuses.

We also need to leave with the sense that this "Journey of Faith and Grace" is finally in the hands of a Provident God who alone knows why and what will follow.

Sincerely and with a continued loyalty to ECC," [signatures]"

Silence followed the letter. The words delivered received no response. It was thus that I went home, empty handed, to begin a new daily ritual.

The new schedule inflicted a very strange syndrome on me. I call it the "Saturday" syndrome. Each day I awaken to "Saturday". No longer does the day begin with Mass at break of day, first coffee and quiet time at 7:30 am in the office, and opening the door of 532 to greet the students and faculty who find their way to that place where coffee and counseling are gifts of body and spirit. Then, home later that afternoon.

Rather, now I rush to a dated pill box to discover the day of the week. It is my marker, the assurance that today is, in fact, not Saturday at all. My new days are flavored with other activities, a still unappreciated retirement from the old ritual, I awake with "Nothing to do today! Must be Saturday!"

Retirement! A "withdrawal from one's occupation"! This suggests that some kind of change will happen in one's daily life, in the rituals that propel us through the day. It certainly has meant that for me. And, for me that also means I have to conquer the Saturday syndrome. I pray that Jesus will call me, urge me to follow him where he wants me to go.

A friend sent me a prayer of "Acceptance". In part it read:. "When I receive the willingness to surrender [to change], I feel free... I realize the only things over which I have any control are what I think and what I do. Daily prayer for the knowledge of God's will...and the power to carry that out, help me to realize that the only certainty in life is change.

Why would I want to clutter my day with resistance? When I am open-minded, ready to listen, and willing to go to any lengths, the solution- God's will for me- appears."

I reflect on some fishermen, a tax collector, some mothers, and women with their daily ritual responsibilities, and how they left all to follow Jesus when he beckoned. How did they leave? How did each take the steps away from his former busy life? Scripture tells little except...they followed him.

Did they also write a letter of resignation to family or friends? Or, was theirs a different "resignation", an acceptance? Alone! Each accepted leaving behind some unnoticed, un- thanked past effort. Each surrendered to change.

We read the story and we see the result of their "retirement". Now, no days were the same as they walked with Jesus. Places, activities, people they met as they journeyed with him now belonged to the unexpected not some planned eight to four familiar day.

When we read that Jesus had nowhere to lay his head, where did these intimate followers now lay their head? And when they awoke what day was it for them?

A TEACHER'S REWARD

Are you a teacher? Have you had to introduce yourself in the middle of a school year? Have you had to look at the sad faces of students whose favorite teacher was being replaced by this unknown nun? Has anyone ever given you an award for tackling such a situation? They say the teacher's reward is usually unseen, hidden somewhere in the achievements, accomplishments, in the developing history of former students' lives

Well, Mahonoy City (pronounced MA-Ha-noy) experienced my arrival in January 1969, yes, the middle of the school year! This Junior Novice was replacing the seventh grade teacher who was leaving.

I arrived at the convent on Mahonoy St. (but pronounced the more familiar MA- noy) where I joined three other sisters. The massive building must have housed many more than four in the days pre-Vatican II. Now sisters were leaving teaching, moving into new ministries and convents seemed larger in their absence.

I was happy to get to the school, St. Canicus, and meet my 7th graders and other students. It is always a bit harder to replace someone than to begin new. How would I break into the space where a favorite teacher once sat at the desk? January was a time to review for semester finals. This review time allowed us to meet in a less demanding time. And, we entered the transition.

Soon we began to resume a daily schedule of subjects including reading which I taught to 6th, 7th, and 8th graders. But, it soon became clear that poor St. Canicus did not have appropriate or sufficient readers for the levels required.

A money gift! The principal announced the gift and asked for suggestions for its use. Immediately my hope was for readers and my hope was answered. After some thought, I found my answer in the SRA Reading Lab.

I prodded the interest of the students, enticed these young people, bound to this coal town, about the world that would open up to them- and, all in a box of reading cards.

To begin, we fussed over the answer books they must create since the gift only bought the Lab. Each brought in the designated "composition notebook", followed instructions, inch by inch, to make up answer sheets. There must always be three answer sheets when one selected a reading card. A success! Perhaps, in this intimate preparation- teacher and student, another success was that the former teacher's face slipped from their memory.

And so, students entered into a new experience of reading and into a world of experiences beyond Mahonoy City. In this place, the sound of fire engines alerted them to the number of bells sounded, bells which identified if their home was in a safe area. Now, reading cards alerted them to areas they might never experience. They were free to imagine and to enter a new world tucked away in the SRA Lab box.

The students grew fond of the Lab. When absent, it was common for students to urge moms to call for cards to be brought to them. Reading was on the rise!

Our sisters left St. Canicus that year. The lack of sisters called us back to other ministries. After all there were three schools in little Mahonoy. St. Canicus would be transferred to the care of another congregation. So, at the close of the year, we packed all class items into cupboards and closed the doors.

My 7th graders invited me to their graduation the next June. The class had become very special to me in the six months I spent with them. I was proud of their achievement and my congratulations to each was a moment of tearful sentiment.

The new principal approached me with a question. "I understand there was an SRA Reading Lab in your classroom. It wasn't in the closet. Where did you put it?"

As I drove home that evening, I wondered which student or students had claimed the SRA Reading Lab as their own. While I pondered that question, I realized that my students had just rewarded their teacher. They were offering me an unspoken "thanks".

Do teachers ask for thanks? Scripture reminds us of the many times that the teacher Jesus met people in their need. Some were blind, some crippled, some tugged at his garment, some asked him to help others who were sick or even dead, some suffered spiritual death, some were hungry while he spoke with them, and some needed to make a catch of fish.

We can picture those scenes and how Jesus gifted each by his response to their need. The scenes are alive with the excitement of those who received the gifts. We see them proclaiming joy for the restoration to health or life or to the satisfied hunger. But thanks?

Remember the ten lepers who were healed? Nine never returned to offer thanks. This is the one time Jesus asks why. His reward was found in the one who did say thanks. Perhaps the joys expressed by others were unspoken thanks.

No students came forward to say thanks. Yet, some were rejoicing in the gift of reading brought to their classroom, signs of their unspoken thanks.

SAILING, SAILING

Have you ever spent time sailing? And do you have a first tale of your first, and perhaps only, sailing experience?

Another friend and I, teased by a beautiful summer day and by friends who had campers along the Canadian shores of Lake Erie, set out for the camp grounds.

How good to bask in the sun over iced tea and diet pop, and in the company of good friends.

As we chatted, Judy invited me to see her two passenger sail boat. Judy lived a very active life beyond her formal career- teacher of history. A bowling ball, golf clubs…these were the tools of her recreation. Now in her camping milieu, she proudly presented her sailing craft.

It was resting on the sandy beach front and its sails stood tall as though ready to venture into the swift moving water. So, when Judy extended her invitation to include a ride in her vessel, I accepted. A sailing novice, I listened as Captain Judy introduced me to a rudder, its importance and when to move it to one side or another. My Captain would control the sails.

And so it was that Lake Erie welcomed the boat into her wet embrace. Soon she was Captain. Now, Judy, as if yielding to being co-captain, was issuing her rudder friend some orders to control us from moving too far from the camp.

You might guess that I, the novice boater, became less than capable of responding to the orders. The sailboat began to drift too far out and to sail in circles. My Captain shouted out her orders to no avail. I watched as the campers on shore and the two chatting friends became more and more distant.

"Why worry?" I called to My Captain. "If things go too bad, we can swim ashore". This went over like a lead anchor, which by the way we didn't have on board. My distressed Captain was not a happy boater. Rather, she was not happy with her rudder friend.

No, we did not have to recourse to a swim. Perhaps, I became a kind of heroine as my rudder efforts brought us back safely.

Once more on shore, I wondered about the anxiety of my Captain. After all the most that might be lost in our uncontrollable situation was the sailboat. We both knew how to swim and though we were far from the camp, we were not lost in the middle of the lake. I surmised it was "swimmable".

As the sun began to hide behind the rippling waters of Lake Erie, so did our thoughts and concerns hide behind some laughter as we reflected on the afternoon from the safety of four beach chairs.

Later and alone, I paused to reflect on Jesus, our Captain. I pictured him among his Apostles, many who were boaters, fishermen by trade. Often, he was on the shore, teaching and yes, even calling out orders.

Remember the day Peter saw Jesus on the shore? Jesus called out to him and Peter responded by leaving the boat to walk out toward his Captain. But, something happened. We think the worse and say he didn't have enough faith to continue the walk or that he was afraid. That conjecture about Peter's failure is not certain. Do we hear that he got wet, that he tried to swim?

What we do hear is that Jesus, the Captain, took over in this time of weakness.

I think that we who control the rudders in our lives, who sometimes fall into the rippling waters of our situations, need to look for Jesus who is either on the shore urging our movements or near us on our boats asking us to respond to his call. Our Captain will lead us into places where we can be safe...either from the shore or as fellow traveler on the boat.

When I think of that day on the Lake I now picture life- a sail boat made for two passengers- Jesus, my Captain calling out orders and me, the rudder mover. We are sailing along together. I can trust that when I move the rudder to one side or another, or make mistaken movements, my Captain is there controlling the sails.

RED DOLLARS & GREEN LEAVES

Remember penny candy? Kids could go to the store with their pennies and find their favorites like licorice straps, bit o honeys, necco wafers, tootsie rolls, wax bottles or candy buttons. And, often the choice might include gummy red dollars or chewy green leaves.

Well, we weren't kids anymore and candy had long lost its place on the shelf marked "penny". In truth, my two best friends and I were of the college ilk. The only thing we had in common with familiar penny candy was a kind of tradition shared only by this trio. How it began is even lost with the years.

For some reason, the combination of red dollars and green leaves became the antidote for any ailment that might befall one of us. I can imagine other non medical antidotes used in families. The script might include ice cream or promises of some other treat. But there was something special about our antidote. It grew into a ritual bond, an expectation for a certain cure or at least of the assured arrival of the other two candy bearers for a visit.

While red dollars and green leaves was our ritual price of entry into the sick bay, the real deal was friendship. Gummies and chewies were only an outward sign. Then just as the penny candy disappeared from candy shelves, our ritual bond seemed to slip away. What remained was the real bond- three people experiencing years of rich friendship and often at a different price.

Now the price was raised. We found that our visits called us to a new patience, a new response to illness that could not be cured by red dollars and green leaves. One of us had been suffering physical diminishment for years. We entered her final sick bay where a new ritual was emerging. Our visit with the gift of a clown doll brought a smile of delight but never the miracle of the penny candy antidote. At other times we swabbed her lips with lemon water, held her fragile hand and whispered prayers as she lay silent, often not knowing we were there.

Fleeting thoughts of college gals bringing healing with penny candy pills are now mingled with the reality of a dying friend. But I kept one of those gift clowns and remember how it was an antidote if only for the brief moment of joy it offered.

Interesting that there are these little rituals that are shared between people that become a defining moment, that create bonds in a relationship. I suspect that we each have experienced such moments and cherished them at least for a time.

I turned to Scripture to search for such non sacramental rituals. A story opened for me- about the three magi who came from the East bringing gifts of gold, frankincense and myrrh. They entered a stable of birth, not of illness or death. The rich gifts were offered almost as an antidote to the lowly place where the child lay on a bed of straw. The gifts offered by Kings to the Divine King. Who could imagine how that simple ritual, that admission of royal birth, would be lost as the child grew into the suffering servant. And, what of that trio of visitors? Would they find their way back to repeat that moment of revelation?

We read of Jesus who went about teaching, healing and unrecognized as the expected Messiah. Scripture reminds us that he had no where to lay his head. It tells us how he was rejected even in his home town. Then, we hear something that takes us back to that royal ritual. A woman, recognizing that he was denied the hospitality of foot washing, pours perfumed oils over his head, washes his feet and dries them with her hair. Perfume, not water! A rich gift, an unnoticed ritual? An expression of anointing, a revelation of another anointing!

As the Jesus story continues, those who accompanied him began to express a concern for his well being. If his kingship was lost on them, his diminishment at the hands of Pilate was thrust upon them- the crown of thorns, the harsh walk bearing the cross, the nails, his death, the burial.

Images of the ritual that greeted Jesus at his birth place, repeated in Simon's house, now move into that place where his body lay. Some women friends and Nicodemus entered and offered him in death a final anointing. Once more perfumed oils, once more myrrh, once more a ritual of kingship and love. In this burial place a sense that the magi ritual was being repeated.

TABLE 36

I approached the table. Sitting alone was a man intent on reading the program for the evening. I sat down opposite him at the round table-table 36. I broke his concentration with an "Ahem!" and a humorous remark: "Well, it looks like you are lucky to have me sitting with you. What's your name?"

But I am ahead of myself. The evening began with other words,

In fact, the words came on a presidential invitation: You are invited to attend the 100th Anniversary dinner as a guest of the President of d'Youville College. I made a call to her office to offer my RSVP- Yes, I will be attending the dinner. Unknown to me, these words were also the beginning of God's Providential movement, when using crooked lines he was leading me straight to table 36.

Now, weeks later, I found myself amid the crowds of people who were gathering in the restaurant lobby. Soon I discovered that I was not registered, that I did not have a seating number. Nor did I have the red guest rose. But not to worry they indicated, there is room at table four.

While I waited for a drink (Pepsi of course), a woman approached me. She said I looked familiar and introduced herself as Cher from the d'YC publication office. But, no, we did not know each other. When I offered my name, and told her my plight, she insisted on investigating the situation. She returned with the information (and a red rose) that I should sit at table 36, not 4, because there would be a woman there that I know and would be comfortable with.

The man at table 36 responded with "My name is Ed." When I told him that I was Sr. Ruth, a Grey Nun, he stunned me when he knew my last name. How was that possible? He was employed at d'YC and had seen my name on a list, and had tried to reach me unsuccessfully some years ago.

That was part one! A coincidental meeting? The next revelation assured me that everything that had happened, that had brought me to table 36 was no accident.

How would you react had an apparent stranger said you were classmates in the fourth grade- sixty four years ago?! Me? I was absolutely overwhelmed as this piece of my past began to unravel with names and memories of those long ago school days!

Ed offered another revelation: "I never attended a special function of the college… it is my first in twenty years."

Everyone at table 36 shared our exhilaration and the wonder of an unexpected meeting of two former, now senior, classmates. The anniversary dinner became for me a reunion surprise party! And, that party was at the invitation of the Providence of God.

Yes, I believe God invites us on journeys to times, places or situations we do not expect. Nor do we necessarily understand the route he takes to bring us to our "table 36".

My thoughts picture Mary, the young Jewish girl and the angelic "ahem!" as he announced his presence and God's invitation to her. Not knowing where her "yes" would lead her, this teen age girl heard the words and accepted. The promise that the Holy Spirit would come upon her was spoken and the angel departed from her.

Now what does a teen age girl do? There were no more directions given. We know the difficulty that beset her immediately. Her relationship with Joseph could have been jeopardized. But Scripture names Joseph a just man and he took Mary as his wife.

Mary's journey had begun. It was a crooked line flowing from a visit to her cousin Elizabeth, the need to reply to a census and give birth in a stable, settling into a carpenter's home for the next thirty years mothering the "Son of God". When her son left his carpenter's tools behind, Mary walked with him still unaware of God's will for her let alone for her son. How did she know that a wedding need for wine could be satisfied by her son? Yet, the mother acted and her response ushered in the beginning of Jesus' ministry.

Was Mary proud of her son as she accompanied him and saw the power that flowed from him? What mother might not be invigorated by the goodness of her child's concern for the sick, the lame, the blind, the dying, those overcome by demons? Were these happy moments for Mary?

Then, the tide of appreciation turned to derision. Now Jesus, her "Son of God", was given a crown, was beaten and forced to carry the cross that would soon bear him- nailed, thirsting, dying.

Was this the place to which a Providential God had led Mary? Was this the sorrowful end…her table of suffering and commission?

She heard the final words. Did they exhilarate her? "Woman behold thy son. Son behold thy mother." Here, standing near the cross, Mary reached the place where God had been leading her. Here she might be remembering how thirty three years ago she said yes…I am the handmaid of the Lord.

A PADDLING PAIR

Remember when New York boasted two baseball teams? The Yankees and the Dodgers! It was the Yankees and the M&M era of Mantle and Maris with a touch of Berra that attracted our foursome. We were four friends frequently on the road to cheer them on.

Our ventures also found the four of us on the road looking for other entertainment and places to see and experience, and there was also our home town and it's invitations that lured us.

We were more than spectators at sports. Our athletic triumphs were lauded on the softball diamond, basketball court, bowling lanes, at table tennis, on a swim team. We played and sometimes we coached. This athletic spirit found us, one day, at Ellicott Creek and an experience of canoeing, my first

So it was that I stepped into a canoe with Annie. The other two, sisters, were likely to partner when twos were in order such as at cards, backseat driving, team events, or as today, in canoes.

My canoe partner and I began this novice experience without rules or directions.

We began our attempt to conquer the still waters of the creek using the tools offered us- paddles. Soon we realized that the paddles seemed not to know how to steer us. We were still near the shore while the other paddling pair moved on and were encouraging us to follow. "What fun!" they shouted.

Fun indeed! After a full circle, our paddles were taking us back to the shore. They seemed not to care that there was a huge tree branch in view. A tree branch boldly stretching its arm away from the bank! A tree branch that seemed to be beckoning us forward, toward it and the bank!

How does one resist what seems inevitable? Aware of our plight, the other canoeers called out directions. But our disoriented paddles, our inexperience, teemed up against this paddling pair. A strike! Paddles were dropped and our hands lifted to protect us from the shoots of foliage that caught us up in their green web.

Picture the final scene! The canoe rolled over and emptied its passengers into the dirty creek waters. After a short underwater flaying we rose and swam to the bank and dry land. But, my penny loafers, my precious Bass Weejuns, were left behind, an unintentional gift, the cost of the creek for disturbing her waters.

Our next road trip took us from the creek site to our home neighborhood, Annie and I in the traditional back seat. The difference now was that we were sopping wet and I was shoeless. At my street corner, I slipped out of the car for the final leg of our day, the barefoot walk to my house.

Water, paddles, canoe and friends! They certainly are words used to describe the episode experienced at Ellicott Creek!

Water, fish, boats, fisherman…one might see just the words. But the words conjure up some events in the activities of Jesus and his disciples and of the stories told in Scripture.

Because they were fisherman by trade Peter and some disciples knew about the water and fishing boats. They were accustomed to storms. They knew about a good catch and had experienced empty nets. Their friend Jesus seemed to be nearby to direct them on those bad days.

Wasn't it he who calmed the storm? And he who encouraged them to drop their nets for a catch? Yet, even responding to Jesus' call, Peter started out only to lose balance and fall into the water.

But the story ends there, not offering a resolution. Did he swim to the shore to finally reach Jesus? Oh, we know he must have finally reached dry land, finally approached Jesus with belief, accepted his direction to "feed my lambs". But there on his cross, was he barefooted as he walked where Jesus beckoned- "to my Father's house"?

A BAD DAY

We had gathered, this small group of friends, in my 2nd floor flat on St. Florian's Street. The gathering was as comfortable with the people as was this space, my home that welcomed them.

I had moved into the flat after our community of four sisters lost the house down the street which we had rented from the parish. The sold sign meant we had to disburse to other residences. A neighbor made me an invitation to consider the upper flat of his home. It was a good place with its living room windows receiving the bright afternoon sun and the porch offering a place for a cool evening comfort space. There was also a small room off the living area which served as a chapel, a place of holy respite.

The occasion was a birthday party with the traditional strains of "Happy Birthday" followed with cake and ice cream, gifts and laughter. I can hear Bruce leading the song, see his wife Karen serving up the goodies and Lorraine handing them first to their three children. Our adult chatter left us unaware of the children- Theresa and Lenika age seven and Clarissa age five, as they skirted about doing kid things together. A fun time! Yes, a good day.

Together! At some point Lorraine became aware that Clarissa was not in sight. Kids like poking around so we checked bedroom and bath. No Clarissa. Might she have wandered onto the porch alone, a not child safe place? No? Another fear was that she might have gone downstairs, onto the street. Our party rushed down but returned without the child.

One last place, the chapel! A peek into the dimly lit room revealed the little girl sitting and looking up at the crucifix affixed to the wall in the corner behind the door. Our burst into the room turned her glance from the crucified Christ to us, the intruders. "Jesus sure had a bad day!" she exclaimed softly. And her mother embraced the child she had been searching for.

We all took a deep breath and welcomed Clarissa back into the party fold. We had taken her from her meditation into the other mood, the one that had gathered us to celebrate.

We can echo Clarissa's lament, "Jesus sure had a bad day!" Somehow the child had wandered into that presence where a plaster image of a bleeding Jesus was affixed to a dark wooden cross. And we caught her in her meditation prayer. Not unusual that she, a little child, was drawn to that place where she would see Jesus. Scripture reminds us of children who seemed drawn to Jesus and the assurance of his welcome.

But, at the foot of the cross on Calvary stood, the now grown child-mother, Mary.. Mary, now a mother looking up at her suffering son. Perhaps she was thinking of that good day when an angel chorus sang "Happy Birthday" and she welcomed guests who arrived bringing gifts. Her mind might have drifted to the time the child Jesus was lost and how she found him in conversation with scholarly Jews; how she must have embraced him and brought him back to their traveling party and to their home.

Perhaps her meditation now was dark and somber. Yet, even in that melancholy mood, words broke the darkness, filled the intruders of this space of death with hope- "Behold thy son…Behold thy mother." Was there an embrace now? Were all now ready to move on, to celebrate Resurrection?

Was this the embrace destined for all of us, the one that calls us to know Mary and to walk into the arms of our "Mother"?

YELLOWED PAGES

Clutter or treasure!? As I moved through the stages of my life, I often bumped into some treasures hidden among the clutter that was heading toward the trash container. My motto has been look before you toss!

One such experience revealed some yellow pages tucked in an old plastic bag. The contents were snippets of writing, incomplete pieces on yellowed paper with ragged edges, pieces torn from their original spiral binding.

There was one about June. June was a high school friend who lived a street away from me. What was the intention of the unfinished piece that lingered in my care .longer than that original friendship?

The untitled composition began...

> "June Lorraine, that music is giving me a headache! Turn off that dago music". The words flowed from the discordant, husky voice of June's mom, much like coal rumbling down a chute. And, as if to match tremor for tremor, the floor creaked noisily as her clumsy, rocking gait brought her corpulent self to June's room.
> "And you ain't goin' out either!" June gave an embarrassed glance toward her friend who sat beside her on the bed. The other, knowing as friends do, lowered her eyes so as not to meet June's.
> Today was like so many other days in June's life. Everything she loved was denied her. Her friends weren't allowed in the house. Music was taboo....

The single, two sided page revealing a mother daughter relationship ended abruptly, unfinished...I know that I was probably the only friend welcomed by the strict atmosphere of that house near the bend on Crowley Avenue.

Near that piece of paper, another paper larger but as yellow emerged with June's face sketched on it. Another memory! This one outlined in purple by my artistic hand was an "aha"! Yes, this one a simple drawing of my friend.

Where is the June of these pieces? Two good friends, we shared the good and bad of our teen experiences. That ragged edged paper, the simple drawing, also brought back memories of happy times together, sharing teen talk and activities and sometimes intellectualizing about our diverse religious beliefs.

I remember that she married, that the house with harsh memories had new tenants, but that school girl friendship has been gone for over fifty years, has become yellowed, an unfinished story in my life.

Memories written, stored away or lost… remind me of the Scriptures. Were they first written down, grown yellow or tattered by use or storage? Some were unfinished or the authors disputed. Each held someone's experience with God, with Jesus.

What matters is that those yellowed pages became a treasure. Each revelation of a memory has become for us a story not to be idly tossed aside as clutter The pages abound in friendship, indeed of two great covenants..

The memory keepers are long gone. Yet we relish in their stories and realize as we read, or listen, that they too suffered the strict rules of their fathers in faith and of the harsh ruling household of Rome.

Yet, they had each other, friends who walked with each other and with the one whom they would call their Master. He would call them friends, fill their minds with the truths that became their memories and when he was no longer with them, as he promised, the Holy Spirit would be their reminder. They gathered around them those who would believe and the stories were carried to all parts of their world.

Now, we look at pages that record those first writings, the sacred memories. We are thankful for the stories, and for the clean white pages that hold them. And, though not yellowed, the friendship that we have with the Master remains unfinished stories in our lives.

WHALES, WATER AND WHITECAPS

The campus minister works in an environment that is rich with possibility and serendipity. To me, this ministry is a call to be present, be aware, believe that God is at work through me and in spite of me.

This God tale is one that recounts the story of David. Like his biblical counterpart, David is small of stature, the good kid, a youth unnoticed, pursuing his interest in environmental science on a campus located in the inner city.

I came to know David when some of his science club friends suggested that I be one of the advisors on their whale watch excursion to Cape Cod. I was personally excited about the idea of whale watching, so I packed my bag and joined this group of budding scientists. We returned enriched by our experience at sea and our new found friendships. This was played out by their frequent visit to the Campus Ministry Center, Room 275.

And, when David dropped by one day, I threw out my traditional question aimed at Catholics: "Have you made your confirmation?" (Somehow I forgot to ask if he was Catholic.) An accidental question! He said he didn't know. But on another visit David said he was never baptized. My role as evangelizer prompted me to ask him to think about attending our RCIA (Rite of Christian Initiation of Adults) / confirmation sessions here on campus.

David faithfully attended each session. When we spoke about God's love for His people, David added his concern for the animal world and the environment. All his references to God's love seemed centered there. Often, Matthew, my associate in the RCIA sessions and I wondered how we could direct his interest to God's people. In the end, we admitted that our role was to plant the seeds, God's role was to water and nurture David.

Thus David came to the waters of baptism, and he accepted the gift of the Holy Spirit in confirmation. Now I became aware of the power that flowed from God into David's spirit. I imagine the life of grace in us is like the whitecaps that form as a wave that crests. Those whitecaps began to be obvious in David's new life. He became a very generous volunteer, doing tedious jobs for me in the ministry. He promoted environmental issues as well as social justice concerns; he participated in retreats and the March for Life in Washington, D.C. All merited David my nomination for the St. Joseph's Award presented to him by Bishop Head at a Diocesan Service.

One day, David questioned me about the Grey Nun associates when he saw one of our brochures. I explained briefly, and David responded swiftly by becoming a member. He studied the life and mission of St. Marguerite d'Youville, founder of the Grey Nuns, and his wave crested. God's whitecap was revealed as David proclaimed: "I've never before had a spiritual focus in my life." He was spiritually energized to be and do what St. Marguerite had by her example been to many – the loving example of Jesus to anyone in need. Soon, David could be heard saying: "Wouldn't it be great if there were brothers who carried on St. Marguerite's spirit – Grey Brothers of the Sacred Heart!" That name, and maybe the idea, was catchy to me. But for David, his wave was swelling to another crest.

Then, God provided another grace. Not only did that interest grow for him, but David searched for, contacted, and was interviewed concerning religious life. At this writing, David is in the Bronx working and living alongside the Christian Brothers serving some of God's needy kids. He'll be back soon. He will contemplate his experience. Perhaps David will become a brother, maybe he won't. But God is at work in his life, and David is listening and growing.

As campus minister, I feel graced to have been present to see God's Providence, His work, unfold. There are many tales to tell when I look back at the past 12 years on campus – most not as dramatic as this one. But I do believe that God is busy in our bit of space at this inner city college campus, whether I noticed those whitecaps or not. It is with this assurance that I mark the beginning of my 13th year as campus minister.

———————————

Continued twelve years later, 2008...

An accidental question! No accident that David is now Brother David, a member of the Missioners of LaSalette. And the whitecaps? They continue as he meets the many calls and challenges of his LaSalette Community.

At David's first profession, I reminded him of that journey from whales to water to whitecaps with a prayer:

> "Whales" he said would open the way, And so we shared whales and water that day. "Water" once more but now called Baptism, You began to see life through a brand new prism. Caught by the Spirit, life would ne'er be the same: "Whitecaps", a God-journey with faith in His name. Today you offer yourself with a pledge of love- A vow of commitment to God above. I'm honored to have walked with you into today. And for our lasting friendship, to You my God I pray.

The words of St. Paul reflect the experience, the humility that an RCIA team is confronted with. His words might be paraphrased:

What, after all is Matthew? And what is Ruth? Only servants, through whom David came to believe- as the Lord has assigned each to his task. We planted the seed, watered it, but God made it grow. So neither he who plants nor he who waters is anything, but only God, who makes things grow.

But, Paul was himself a convert. He realized the power of God's grace. He put aside his old life to be an apostle of Jesus, to carry His message. The overwhelming change in his life began with a question- not accidental, but God's: "why are you persecuting me?" He had to answer the question. After his brief instruction, his RCIA, he was ready to take on the "whitecaps" that would change him as much as the message he would carry, the seed he would plant.

Thus, from the question comes the heroic response that meets the challenges required of the message bearer, the seed bearer. He may be called Apostle or Brother.

The "P" Source
A Creative Pen

I love to write and my Gospels and other writings express my creative self.

Each is from my Pen (-ksa).

In the Novitiate, we had an hour affectionately dubbed "forced fun". It was a time to gather as a community. During that time the sisters shared their diverse talents. We had guitar players, polka dancers, singers and actors. When I admitted to none of these talents, someone teased, "Write a Gospel." What emerged from that evening of forced fun was "The Gospel According to the 'P' Source."

Scripture scholars have tried to discover whether Mark was written before Matthew. There arose the possibility of "quelle" meaning source- or "Q", a postulated document related to the Gospels.

Borrowing the idea, the 'P' is the source that identifies my writing. It became a tradition that extended into many situations for entertainment or just to capture an event.

ACCORDING TO THE "P" SOURCE

Introduction to "P"

A theological question was posed: Which was the first Gospel- Mark or Matthew? How can the shorter Mark be first? Most agree that there had to be another source since Matthew's content cannot derive from the shorter Mark. That "source" has been identified as "Q"- quelle which means source.

In the 1950s the Dead Sea Scrolls emerged. These were writings attributed to the Essene community. The teaching Church deemed them as not offering anything beyond the canon of writings which are sufficient for salvation.

Then in 1967 there emerged the "P" source from the Community of Grey Nuns in Yardley of Bucks County. The non-canonical "P" writings are attributed to the postulant Penksa.

Some may be familiar with these heretical writings. Certainly, to take them too seriously might endanger one's salvation. It is well therefore, to consider the basis, the background of each of the three "P" writings offered here.

1. Another Birthday

This reflects the occasion when we celebrated the birthday of a Grey Nun leader during one of our meetings. 2 Feb. 1988 A.D.

In words like those of my brother Jesus, today this Lucan-like gospel is fulfilled in your hearing (Luke 1:26-38, 43, 44 An Annunciation):

In the second month, on the 28th day, some angelic Chapter folks were sent to the town of Pennsylvania named Yardley, to a celibate (the original Latin has it "virgin", but this writer is conservative) vowed to a Congregation named Grey Nuns of the Sacred Heart. The celibate's name was Charlotte. Two days after arriving, the Chapter folks said to her: "Rejoice, O highly favored Superior General! Another birthday is with you. Poor are you among women." She felt an overriding concern for these words and wondered what this option meant. The Chapter folks went on to say to her: "Do not fear, Charlotte, you have found preferential love with God and the materially poor. You shall conceive a mission statement and bear living more simply, working with the poor, educating yourself to the responsibility of justice, acting on societal conditions and you will give it all the name of "preferential love for the poor". Great will be your awareness of our rich heritage of responsiveness and you will be called true daughter of Marguerite. The Lord God will call you to remember that he is the Eternal Father and that our apostolic religious congregation and the Roman Catholic Church must reign together until the end."

Charlotte said to the Chapter folks: "How can this be since I do not know if God is a man?" the Chapter folks answered her: "Divine Providence will come upon you and the desire to collaborate will overshadow you, hence the holy mission statement to be born will increase the influence of Gospel values in the world. Know that other Grey Nuns, your kinswomen, have received the same message in their old age; they who were thought to be rejecting solidarity with the poor are now in the advanced months of the process, for nothing is impossible since Vatican II."

Charlotte said: "I'm simply celebrating my birthday today. So let's be done with this stuff!" With that the Chapter folks had to agree. When they heard Charlotte's greeting, they called out in a loud voice: "Young are you among women and blessed is the fruit of your term. Glad are we that the "Mother" of our Congregation should celebrate her birthday with us today." This is good news!

2. The Discernment Process 1993

This important gathering of Grey Nuns was a time to elect our leadership for the next five years. For this purpose we were to use a discernment model. This model, like many, included a vocabulary that would lead us through a process whose end was the nomination and election of Sisters who would serve the congregation as our Leadership Council. Thus, according to "P" in the style of Matthew:

Matt.1:18 according to "P" - The Birth of the Discernment Model.

Now, this is how the birth of the discernment process came about.

When members of the Chapter '93 planning committee came together to "debrief", and after reading Superior General Jean's letter, they were empowered by the spirit of the facilitator's presentation for the selection of our Grey Nun leaders.

The committee, an upright group of sisters, willing to focus on the fact that "Love Changes Everything", decided to think about it quietly. Such was their intention when suddenly the answer of the Lord appeared in a "Dream Dreams" prayer saying: Chapter committees, daughters of Marguerite, have no fear about "Gathering the Dreamers". You will bear this Chapter and you are to name its graces- diminishment, conversion and discipleship.

All this happened to fulfill what had been said in the prophetic reading: "Dreams will come and go in our lives. But, what beauty can be experienced as we accept the challenge of a dream!" When they awoke to this meaning, they did as the words directed them and received them into their discernment pre-suppositions for leadership. The committee had a lot of relations until the Chapter was born.

Matt.2:1 according to "P" - The Nominations.
After the process birth in Yardley of Bucks County, during the reign of Sr. Eileen, nominations arrived in Yardley, inquiring- are these possible new leaders of the Congregation? We have observed these persons at their best and want to pay them homage.

At this time, Eileen showed concern, and all the committee with her. Summoning the chief counters of the committee, she enquired of them whether the nominees to be considered had the necessary five calls to leadership. Then, here is what she had written:

You, Grey Nun nominees, from all the parts of our land are each our leaders, the ones who will shepherd our Grey Nun trail.

The nominees, who were called, took themselves aside to discern and in the process fourteen names made an appearance. These were sent forth to Holy Redeemer after being instructed: Go in silence, with your tiny vigil lights, to your holy ground of discernment. When you have discerned names to recommend, come back and report all to the Greys at Boniface that they might cast their ballot and ratify the discernment.

At the end of the elections, the sisters were overjoyed that they had found a Superior General and Administrative Board. All sang and gave them blessings. They opened the coffers of their hearts and offered them gifts of peace, joy and love. They continued the message of the "Dream Dreams" prayer: Nothing is impossible if we build our dreams with faith.

And so, all sisters went back to their own states, by route of their LAG (local area government) groups, to fulfill what the Lord had said through their discernment- Out of Philly and New York, I have called a leadership team.

3. The Retirement.
A luncheon and farewell thoughts for Mel, a biology professor about to enter retirement. So, according to "P" in the styles of John, Mark and Luke:

> John 12:20-36 The Last "Luncheon" discourse-
> foretells his career and subsequent retirement.

Among those who went up to celebrate at the luncheon were some colleagues.

These had approached Mel who came from the science department in ECC and put these accolades to him. "Sir, we would like to honor you." So his secretary set out to gather his colleagues and friends.

Mel replied to them:

> Now the hour has come
> for this biologist to be retired.
> I tell you most solemnly
> If a college prof. remains on these ECC grounds till he dies-
> he'd remain only a dead guy.
> But if he retires, he will enjoy a rich experience.
>
> Anyone who loves his job so much is goofy;
> anyone who realizes he has a life beyond this college
> will enjoy that life in the world and prepare for his eternal life.
>
> If anyone knows me, he will agree with my idea cause

wherever I go, you colleagues will soon follow.

Now my soul is not troubled.
What shall I say?
Friends, thank you for this hour.
But it was by reason of many years that I have come to this hour.
Friends, I've enjoyed sharing days here.

A voice came from heaven: "I have glorified your choice, Mel, and I will glorify it again." Colleagues gathered near didn't hear this but agreed, even without a sound of thunder. Some said, Mel's an angel of a biologist and it was for his sake that we came. Mel assured them that it was not only for his sake that the voice came, but also for ours.

Now a giant is passing from our Campus world.
Now a prince of a prof. will leave... on his own.
And when he has departed, who can take his place?
And how will we ever draw another biologist to ourselves?

By these words are indicated our feelings, alive, toward you Mel.
We colleagues say "the law of life has taught us that you'll actually remain in us forever." We can say that because our Mel has drawn so many to himself?

Mel answered:

I'll be with you a little longer now.
Enjoy me while you might
or you'll be in the dark when I go.
While you still have me, believe me, you should take advantage
and you'll have memories for later.

Having said this, Mel went to his lab but did not keep himself hidden.

John 12:44-50 according to "P" -Conclusions
Mel declared publicly:
Whoever remembers me
sees not me in blue or brown
but in the white lab coat I wear.
I the biologist have come into the college

so students, whosoever believe in me,
need not stay in the dark any more.
If students hear my words
but don't study them faithfully,
it is not I who shall fail them,
since I have come not to condemn them
but to ace their academic world.
Students who reject my efforts
have their judge already:
the biology, the anatomy, I have taught
will be their judge on the final exam.

Mark 14:12-16 according to "P" - "Preparations for the "luncheon"
As St. Pat's and St. Joseph's days came around, this campus minister said:
"I am preparing for us to eat from the religious-ethnic tables." So I went into City places to find everything for the preparations. I knew Mel, a man who always brought corned beef and cabbage. When the day arrived and the many guests... all were at the table. Mel said,
I have been happy to prepare this food for you but I shall not do it again after I depart because from now on I will be retired.

Luke 24 according to "P" - The Return Narrative
It was on the first day of the next semester. Some went to the Science lab and they were prepared to find it empty. But, behold they found Mel in his dazzling white lab coat. They were surprised. But he said: I am retired not dead. And then they remembered what he had said to him while still at ECC, that this biologist must retire and then possibly return part time another day.

Then he opened their minds to understand. And he said to them,

Thus it has been with many, that a retiree would depart and come back another day. You are all witness to this so I am offering this promise-you'll stay in the City until you retire and then, some day later return and ascend to your department and be empowered by those on high.

Then Mel raised his hands and blessed us "en nomine patri, et filii, et spiritu sancti.'

We return this blessing Mel.

We do you homage today and hope you go off to retirement with great joy!!!!!

A CONVERSATION WITH GOD
24 November 2001

During the Thanksgiving season the Teen-Share group at my church, moderated by my friend Bruce, sponsored an evening of reflection on the Celebration of Life- the blessing and goodness of life. The specially invited were the physically and mentally disadvantaged.

All gathered as we were called to sing God's praise, to listen to the scriptures, to offer our petitions and thanksgivings.

As part of our celebration of life, I was invited to write a prayer. As I reflected on my task, this is what I wrote:

"A Conversation with God- I heard the Lord call my name"

The word of the Lord spoke to me
and called me from my mother's womb-
    Come with your burdens or infirmity
    Come as you are into my love where there is room.
    Physical or mental challenges you suffer?
    Come to my grace; bring who you are to offer.

My God, what are you saying?
    Did you name me "deaf" or "blind"?
    What name did you give my mind?
    Did you say, you are "No-Legs" or you are "No-Speech"?
    Or, "Never to reach"? Or, "Hard to Learn"?
    Did you call me to struggle while others discern?
    Did you call me "Without arm"?
    Will my caresses seem less warm?

Ah... God spoke,
But you have my Son that you might know
and with Him in my true image grow.
    He is Jesus and he too wondered about His name
    and about all our infirmities that He must claim!
    Oh I love Him, God spoke, as I do you from birth to this very day.
    His name is "His Life", "His sacrifice" too- they are the way!

And how do I answer you, God, I pray?
God simply had this to say...
Remember when doubt is there
that you bear my image, only one life do we share.
That I am with you through it all... always be aware.

CELL-MANIA
A Reflection on presence

I was conscious of Catholics joining many others among the Christian denominations to celebrate the Feast of the Annunciation. This day has been set aside to honor the most awesome moment in human history, when centuries ago in a tiny village called "Nazareth," a very young and unmarried woman said "Yes" to the Angel Gabriel. The Annunciation recalls that incredible day when Mary fulfilled a prophesy, and by physically accepting the Holy Spirit she agreed to become the Mother of God. (*Luke 1:38*)

At one point during my day, still caught up in my thoughts, but a bit overtaken by a momentary gaze away from my computer, I was struck (once again) with the number of cell phone users who pass by my office door. They walk and talk, chatting away, connected mysteriously to some invisible friend or loved one, and (once again, according to my observation) seem so oblivious to the world around them.

Cell phones, I thought: an incredible convenience for some, and an amazing invention, for sure. It's the kind of technology that offers us a reminder of the gifts that God provides through the blessing of human ingenuity.

On the other hand, (still thinking about cell phones) they serve as a caution about a special set of temptations that we all face as human beings. As both "saints and sinners" we tend to isolate our thoughts and to wall ourselves off from others; to hold back and resist interaction with those in our midst; and sadly, to miss out on the chance to interact with a simple greeting, a cost-free smile, or a kindly eye contact.

None of us can ever know how we might be changing another person's bad day by the peace we spread through our simply being "there" with an acknowledgement - like a smile, or a "good morning." Or, just a plain old "hi!"

The cell phone, as wonderful a convenience as it is, can disconnect us from our opportunity to share the most simple and valuable human experience- to be with one another, to brighten another's day, to live out the Commandment. "You must love... your neighbor as yourself." (*Luke 10:27*)

I couldn't help but think about how different history would have been had Mary been busily chatting on a cell phone, oblivious to the presence of the Angel Gabriel, only to have missed the chance to say "Yes" to the Lord.

CIRCLE THE CITY WITH LOVE

An experience of Philadelphia's poor.

We went into the City...to the neighborhood of 9th and Cambria, to circle the city with our love.

Sr. Eileen and I arrived in the City, and in the company of our guide, a social service sister, we walked through the neighborhood. Yes, we came to circle the City with our love. And, the City ignored us. There was no special welcome. Rather, it reached out and embraced us with the same ugly arms that had greeted its tenants that morning, the morning before and...

We were grasped by its arms of brick and concrete- row houses and streets- hot, sweating, without the comfort of trees stretching out cooling limbs to offer shade or to shadow the ugliness of squalor all about. They were arms like those with uncared-for leprosy- blistered, open with the insides pouring out, filthy, broken, a nauseating stench emanating from its sore spots. They were arms pocked by garbage- either bagged or "waiting", or strewn about, marking sidewalk and street with its own gross graffiti.

I felt too clean, a stranger in the midst of this embrace as I walked over bottle caps and broken glass and I moved aside in deference to broken furniture and trash in our path. As I peeled gum from my shoes, the thought of people being "stuck" here tugged at my heart.

Our guide seemed to sing the song to us as we tried to keep up with her rhythm, moving from street to street, door to door, person to person. She offered a loving heart to each person. We listened, we saw.

"Build bridges that unite", the song begins....and we looked at them- people whose lives had known brokenness because of murder, rape, abuse, separation of family members, squalor, insecurity; people with names and faces and stories; people like Ruth, Delia, Gilberto...

"We are the hope for changing stones to bread"...more, we are confronted with the Gospel imperative of love- love that does not offer a stone when the need is bread. Yet, the stone-responses stand here where the need-the bread- is food,

Decent housing, sanitation of homes and streets, education (of rights and opportunities), physical and mental care!

Our guide's song is a living sound that circles the people of St. Bonaventure Parish. Her direct, vibrant, loving presence penetrates the tight grasp of oppression that binds this Hispanic community. When she goes out to meet her neighbors, this sister brings a deep concern for each person, a concern for the person's dignity and integrity unlike those political and social institutions that offer one sided help or those which neglect help completely.

What about our experience of a day with the poor? Sr. Eileen seemed drawn to return to a close bonding with the poor. To her gentle "Mucho gusto", her heart seemed to echo, "Hasta muy pronto". I suppose I am left listening to my heart and I know, even more now, that "Tuesday" assured me of presence "desde los ojos de los pobres".

To those who did not have the experience of our Tuesday with the poor, to those who have not spent time with the materially poor, let us take renewed inspiration from Marguerite d'Youville, from Jesus, from his Sacred Heart.

I am left feeling that some of my prayer must be a litany lived in the street-chapel where the poor pray.

PEACE PRAYER
Offered at the Inauguration of our College President

O god, your creature stands before you this day created in your image to co-create, co-redeem, co-sanctify.

Do I co-create, worship war?
>   Do I romanticize George Washington, Robert E. Lee, Davy Crocket, George Patton, The Contra, and the Sandinistas?
>   What triumphs do I immortalize? Caesar's wars, civil wars, native American struggles, world wars, apartheid, Vietnam, the "just war"?

Do I ignore peace, neglect redemption?
>   Whom do I embrace? Ghandi, Martin Luther King, Dorothy Day, Tolstoy, Jeanette Rankin, Jeanne Vanier, Jesus, St. Francis, Jane Addams, Daniel Berrigan, Bishop Tutu?
>   What triumphs speak to my heart, are redeeming? Those of non-violence? The Salt March in India, the civil rights march of King, the care of a dying person in the hands of Mother Teresa?

Do I sanctify force to solve problems, conflicts?
>   The force of justice, the force of love, the force of sharing wealth, the force of non-violence?
>   Are these the sanctifying essence of my peace, Lord?

Your invitation reaches out to me. The call is a simple one.
>   Build the human family.
>   Provide occasions for humankind to grow.
>   Invite your neighbor to flower and flourish.
>   Create a space where love is, will be- situations where healing takes place.

"Peace I leave with you...
>   Peace is my gift to the world, to this county, this city,
>   the ECC community at North, South and City...
Peace is my gift to you."

O Lord, how shall I be Your channel of peace today? Tomorrow? And tomorrow?

This I pray. Amen.

WILL YOU PRAY FOR ME?
A reflection on intercessory prayer

Sometimes I find little notes asking me questions about faith or religion. One such note turned up at my door. While I prefer to talk person to person so there can be some dialog, I offered this response!

The note asked:"I was wondering where does it say in the bible I should pray to Mary? When I read it, I was told to only pray to God".

I began, Dear Note Writer, There are several parts to a good answer to your question.

First, remember before the bible was written there was an oral tradition. The people of the New Testament who met Jesus knew about him and what he was doing. After the Resurrection, they would tell the stories. Some wrote down the details of an event when they experienced Jesus. Many such scripts were likely written down by people in the various places Jesus visited. The stories were told and retold.

At some point beginning around thirty years later, some collected these stories and wrote down what others remembered. These were gospels. Finally, the Church, finding these gospels and other writings gathered them into what is now the New Testament. It is a compilation of Jesus' mission on earth and of the development of the early church.

Scripture also offers great reverence to Mary. She is called "blessed... among women" and "the mother of my Lord" (Luke 1:42-43), and "all generations will call her blessed" (Luke 1:48), Jesus was obedient to Mary and Joseph (Luke 2:51). She is the only woman named who waited for the Holy Spirit (Acts1:14). What a special place Mary had in the heart of the early Church! No doubt her Son continued to listen to her pleas.

Stories were remembered and retold about Mary. One wonderful story takes place in Cana at a wedding. When the host runs out of wine it is Mary who intervenes and asks Jesus to do something. Jesus does what Mary asks.

Don't we sometimes find others to speak for us? When I was a young girl and wanted to go to the movies, I would go to my brother and urge him: "You ask Mom, she'll listen to you"... We'd get to go to the movies.

Even Martin Luther, well after he had renounced the Catholic Church, spoke in glowing terms about Mary:

> "Here passes the woman who is raised above the whole human race!"... "She was not filled with pride by this praise..." He prayed, "No woman is like unto thee! Thou art more than an empress or queen... blessed above all nobility, wisdom or saintliness!" (From Luther's works) Should I hesitate to approach Mary, to ask her to speak to Jesus in my behalf?

St. Paul speaks of the example of the Apostles and shows that it is good to recognize the holiness of God's saints and imitate them. In Hebrews and Philippians Paul exhorts us to imitate him and the saints for their fidelity and example. So, the practice of turning to these people- to Mary and the Saints is actually very biblical.

I left the written response in the pace where I found the unsigned note.

Now, as I sit at my desk, a student comes in. I don't know her name. She is troubled and she seeks my prayer, my intercession to our God. We hold hands and I pray... to God, to Jesus and Mary for her need.

OUR BEST SELVES
Teachers et al

An article I read recently, "A New Way of seeing", interested me from the point of view of faith and of teaching, of being a student... "...Surge into new life." The words attracted me at once. Our faith calls us to do just that, not surge from nothing but from the roots of our tradition, our Baptism. The Calvarys that we face, suggests the author, can be transformed: we face them with faith and when we do so "we transform them into holy ground".

Now stretch with me a bit. For teachers, this is a new semester. You have lived other semesters and have relied on all that prepared you for another Fall semester, for whatever work you are doing- administration, education, clerical, maintenance, housekeeping. Perhaps you are a student. Here is an invitation to draw from the fountain of your past preparation and experience, your life vocation. Whatever the Calvarys anyone of us may face- irritating colleague, whiny associates, boring or repetitive work, the long commute, disinterested students, boring teachers..."all represent the place to which Christ calls us...the arena where belief becomes action." I suggest with the author, all that has gone before which is sound and has brought you forward thus far, all are the "symbols" which offer you a fresh start "full of vigor and potential.". You come to this academic setting, this arena for action. Yes, our best selves can be renewed, can surge into new life, draw us to "a new way of seeing."

For those not in academia, those in other places of employment- the message remains yours. Perhaps you have not experienced the long summer between June and September. But, you may have paused for a week or two to smell the roses, to waft in the days free of demanding schedules or duties. A return to your work site can be a return to a place where you bring personal renewal. Calvary reappears but so does the action of that place. Even where you must die a bit, you come renewed by the symbols of the past and the grace of faith readied by that simple two week respite. Look at the cross again and see new life- Resurrection!

(Article quotes- "A New Way of Seeing" from EveryDay Catholic July 2005)

WORLD DAY OF PRAYER
6th March 1981 Eden NY

The theme of this World Day of Prayer, 6 March 1981, is "The Earth is the Lord's (and the fullness thereof)". And, if indeed we are to recognize the sorrow of the earth, if we are to be healers of the earth's wounds, if we are to offer worthy gifts of self, if we are to participate in the new earth, then I believe we must be convinced of our affinity, our relatedness, our union with the cosmic creation.

And so I would like to present three scenarios, three reflections, that I hope will convict us of this cosmic reality.

The first takes place in a garden, the second in a potter's house, the third at a Meal.

<u>In the Garden.</u>

It was in the beginning and in the presence of Word and Spirit that a formless void responded and the spectacle of living unfolded, reflecting Diving beauty. All that was, united in a chorus of praise-
> Angels of heaven, virtues of earth,
> stars of the firmament, water and the sea,
> birds and fish and beasts
> rose out of themselves to resemble the Holy.

And God saw that it was good.

Yahweh God said "Let us make man in our own image" and he fashioned man of dust from the soil.

What image is suggested in this creative moment? Out of the mouth of God comes the Word and God's Spirit hovering over the chaos with hope and praise. The creative Word enters the chaos and brings shape, order and beauty to it. God-Word-Spirit, three in one, a community, a unity!

And man? He awakens in a garden with a unique experience of life. He shares the physical, biological life of the earth and its blessing: God saw all he had made and it was very good. Man, in communion with the created world- his body reflects that reality. In the creative act,, man and all creation came in contact with a power beyond them, a force which they can neither cause nor control.

In the Potter's House.

On that 6th day in the Garden, we hear the command of God that this man must be master- a steward, over the creation to which he awakened. Yes, even over the earth from which he was made!

Yet, we need to enter the potter's house with Jeremiah recalling that we are clay and to experience the tension suggested: How are earth and clay both shaper and shaped? I suspect the lesson provided by Jeremiah offers the potter as an example. ...when the vessel he was working at came out wrong he started afresh. Starting afresh may be our cue as stewards, may be the challenge that faces us personally and for the rest of creation. By that example we can imitate the Potter, the one in whose image we are created. We can bring about new earthen vessels where chaos prevails and remake old vessels, bring shape, order, and beauty to them.

The two scenarios reveal that we have a physical relationship to the earth and through that experience we are involved in something beyond only .our own power. We come in contact with life's force- God Creator, Man in his image, and our role as vessel and steward .that preserve what it means to be human. Through them the inner reality of Presence emerges.

At a Meal.

Eating is usually understood in its context of having a meal. It means to enjoy the deliciousness, the fruitfulness of the earth. .Unfortunately, we do not meet our meal, the food, in its original gifting place. We are cut off from seeing it come from its source by wrapping, canning, freezing, etc. Food, the earth gift of life and nourishment!

Having a meal, eating together, is sharing with another this source of life and nourishment and at once creating and nourishing the life of persons- a community. It is in sharing a meal that our lives are grounded with other human beings.

The elements of the meal may be bread, soup, salad, meat, cheese, vegetables, cake, wine... An assortment of these foods is brought into reality and they set up a boundary- such as a fish fry, spaghetti dinner... So we may say there is an organized power to "meal". It assembles the fruitfulness of life and cuts the immense experience to our size allowing us to cope with that immensity. We can thereby experience a part of life in an intense way and by this physical act of eating allow an inner reality to emerge.

There is sacredness, then, even in the way we eat a meal. Festivity and joyousness and gratitude should accompany it. Doesn't it seem almost sacrilegious when one eats too fast, with boorish habits, or wasting what is uneaten?

We entered the theme of this Prayer Day and have paused to consider the harmony evident in our experience of being the Lord's. In this message I have offered a look at the theme through the images of a garden, a potter's vessel and a meal

We have gathered in this place, people united by a faith experience with our God that reaches beyond our being Protestant, Catholic or Orthodox. We have come to celebrate and to worship, to acknowledge our harmony with our Creator God, with all mankind and with the earth.

It is in this cosmic reality that we become ourselves a hymn of glorification:
    All that is,
    what speaks and is silent
    All declare You-
    All that is
    What thinks and what cannot think
        All praise You!
    The world-desire,
    The world-sighing,
    Move toward You.
    Your world sends up to You
    A hymn of silence...

The earth indeed is the Lord's, and the fullness thereof!!!

WHO TOLD YOU THAT?

A student offered his article for me to read and share.
Because of "slam Buffalo people" the first words irritated me
but he urged me to read on...Now, I urge you to "read on"!

"Buffalo, you wouldn't catch me there, it's freezing, all it does is snow, and it's dirty, the summers are boring and nothing ever goes on there. It's not my kind of town."

Wait a minute, you pessimist. I've got some news for you. The City of Buffalo and surrounding areas are brimming with entertainment from the cold winter days to the hot summer nights.

This is one of the most entertaining cities in America. Buffalo's not that dirty frozen block of ice that people are led to believe. This is a town with a cornucopia of power packed activities and a wonderful, positive use of each of the four seasons. Id like the chance for those misguided souls to be here right now with their erasers, so they can rub out the negative thoughts they probably heard from someone, who heard it from someone else, and so on.

Living here for (48) years, I have heard and read so many negative things about my city, it has gotten to the point that it is sometimes amusing to hear the put downs. Even as I sit quietly writing this by the shores of Lake Erie, I feel the cool spring breeze coming off of it. Adding some color to my scenic pleasure is a great ship gliding effortlessly down the canal on its way to somewhere. It is almost like a page out of Samuel Clemens' book "Huckleberry Finn".

Winter.

Yeah, we get winters, and like some other cities it's cold and snowy, but what are you going to do, lock yourself up in your house? Winters are fun if you utilize them right. People actually travel up from the south to ski and hunt here. Buffalo and the surrounding areas have quite the reputation of having some of the best skiing in the country. I've been to a couple of the resorts around here and have found them to have a four star rating. As far as hunting, whitetail deer are plentiful.

Summer.

Buffalo summers are the best you can find anywhere in the northeast. Here is a great deal of anticipation for their arrivals. When they do get here, watch out! This city blooms. It always brings on great wonder to me as I watch summer unfold in front of my eyes. Flourishing trees and beautiful flowers are just a little part of nature coming back to life and with it a refreshing and new feeling. Anyone lucky enough to be here for the change of season will attest to this. Buffalo surely knows how its arrival with a huge number of events and gatherings that last through the summer. And, I'll tell you my friend, these bashes are second to none.

Buffalo is the starting and finishing point for many shipping tasks. It has been for over a hundred years [note our marinas and a popular Marina Park downtown with opportunities to go aboard a real ship docked there or on other visiting ships].

Buffalo has quite a selection of entertainment offerings in the summer months, and most are free or very affordable and many in or near your own "backyard". As gas prices skyrocket, you'll be pleased to know that some are only a short drive away. With such a variety of entertainment, I am sure even the toughest critic can be pleased.

Do you like music? There are concerts offered in different locales and times and kinds in the city and nearby as well. In Lewiston, just outside Buffalo, we have Art Park- a full multi-cultural entertainment center that offers a dynamic lineup of free concerts on select evenings with heavier hitter artists such as The Glenn Miller Orchestra, the band "Blood, Sweat & Tears and various blues artists. With

Different ages of music represented throughout the summer, you're sure to find something to suit your taste.

Art Park also offers arts and crafts and theatre, for the whole family, so you can plan to spend the day.

Closer to Buffalo are the Tonawandas' Gateway Park. This fully renovated facility is situated on the mouth of the historic Erie Canal. It offers a mix of history, beauty and music. The result: another reinforcing reason why you should be thankful you're in Buffalo. It is wonderful that our contributing neighbors can offer free music. That's what I call getting an affordable earful as well as an enjoyable view.

Right here in Buffalo, music lovers can enjoy a Sunday summer afternoon without even reaching into their pockets. Our city proves that we offer all tastes and styles of music by offering live jazz concerts on the steps of the Albright Knox Art Gallery, revered as one of the most popular galleries in the world. In my opinion "art never sounded so good". (Yes, the gallery itself provides an all season offering]. You have to admit there is a double hitter right there! How many home runs do we have so far? [and what about our teams throughout the seasons...baseball, basketball, football... college and pro offerings!] I have lost count.

I could sit here and offer numerous other entertainment examples offered through Buffalo's lively and colorful seasons, but there are too many. To be honest with you, I would rather you see them for yourself! Music and plays already mentioned [and Studio Arena, Sheas, Irish Theatre... and more], fairs [garden walks], carnivals, [festivals:[, and how about the Eden Corn Festival? renowned Allentown Art festival...myriad home food experiences- wings, roast beef on weck... and those little [and popular] ice cream shops down the street [Antoinette's...sponge candy anyone? Anderson's ...]

The fullness we experience in our city with the changing seasons and how we make the best of them makes us strong [versatile] and receptive to the joys that have been bestowed upon us here.

This city- Buffalo- opens wide its arms, all year, every year, and wide enough to take you in with hospitality and a richness that, possibly, you have never felt in another city. Hopefully. I can speak for all of us [Buffalonians] when I say, "Come to us. Let us embrace you". After you have spent some time here, you may find it painlessly acceptable to change your way of thinking toward us and surprisingly [admit], "Buffalo, I've been here, it is fantastic! The people are warm and the seasons beautiful...I cannot wait to come back!"

Written by a student with editions noted in [ ].

KNOW HIM BY HIS NAME:

The name of the Lord is a strong tower; the
righteous runs into it and is safe.
Proverbs 18:10

"What's in a name", the poet asked. The Jews of biblical times believed that knowing a person's name was to know the person. A name represented the person- his character, his attributes, his very nature.

Perhaps the name of God most are familiar with, the name most frequently used in the Old Testament, is *Jehovah* or commonly rendered as *Yahweh*. The name is derived from the Hebrew root which means "to be or to become." The name, then, speaks to God's being or essence. It is a reference to the One who is totally self-existent.

Jesus speaks of the One who "has life in Himself." John 5:26. The humanists say, "Where is God? Who made God? How did God come into existence? Everything must have a cause. So, God had to have a cause. God had to come into existence at some time.

And, how does one respond to these faithless outcries? In a word! That word is the very name of God- *Jehovah/ Yahweh*. His name says, "I always have been, I always am, and I always will be." Moses received this truth when he wondered about the commission laid upon him. He was about to learn the limitless power of a single name when he asked, "Whom shall I say sends me?"

Moses said to God, "Behold, I am going to the sons of Israel,
and I shall say to them, 'The God of your fathers has sent me to you.'
Now they shall say to me, 'What is His name?' What shall I say to them"?
And God said to Moses, "I AM WHO I AM" and He said,
'Thus you shall say to the sons of Israel, 'I AM has sent me to you...
Thus you shall say to the sons of Israel.
'The Lord, the God of your fathers, the God of Abraham,
the God of Isaac, and the God of Jacob, has sent me to you.'
This is My name forever; and this is My title to all generations." Exodus 3:

God chooses to identify Himself to us, that is, to reveal Himself to us in all that His person is, by His name.

Consider the first time you and I are introduced to God in the pages of the Bible. We are introduced to Him by the name, in the Hebrew language, *Elohim. In the beginning God- Elohim- created the heavens and the earth.* Genesis 1:1

The Spirit of God was moving over the surface of the waters,

Then God said, "Let there be light"; and there was light. Genesis 1:2-3

El means mighty or strong. The *-him-* ending is plural. Then, is there more than one God? No. In Deuteronomy 6:4 we read: "the Lord [Yahweh] is our God [Elohim], the Lord is one!" God the Father, God the Son, and God the Holy Spirit- the Blessed Trinity- created the heavens and the earth. God is one in essence yet the different roles or persons of his character participated in the work of creation. Later, God [*Elohim*] says 'Let us make man in Our image.' Genesis 1:26.

As we come to know God, it is interesting to let Him reveal the fullness of His personhood by learning to use His name, and to call upon Him by His particular name. If you wish to know God by His other names, you may want to browse through a book: To Know Him by Name by Kay Arthur.

By the way, how many names do you have? Mine are: Ruth, Sister Ruth Marie Penksa gnsh, Aunt Ruthy, great Aunt Ruthy, Cousin Ruth, Sis, Rudee...friend!

DEFACERS NOT WELCOME

A response to faceless "Que"

It is sad that, in this country of ours, where freedom abounds, even students who speak with non-American accents, who like to be respected for their culture or beliefs, have not heeded the words of our Constitution. In this case, the precious words are "freedom of religion".

My comment follows the ignorant action by a student whose only signature is "Que?". Campus Ministry has a policy of recognizing the holy days of the religions practiced by our diverse community here on the Campus.

When Campus Ministry placed Ramadan information flyers on the table outside the office, a student chose to mark up one sheet and slip it under the Campus Ministry office door. Scrawled over the Ramadan text was a cross. At the top of the cross was the signature "Que?" and at the bottom, the words "In God We Trust".

I suppose the ignorant artist was trying to send his "born again" message not out of respect for others but out of the spiteful hammer of intolerance and righteousness!!! And the spoiler had to do it without admitting who he/she was.

Well my brother or sister, you are not the first to condemn someone's point of view. By chance, is your name Judas?? I don't see your face.

So "Que?", or Judas, or whatever your name, what I have to say to you is GO HOME! Go home if you cannot tolerate material that describes another American's religion or customs. GET OUT OF THIS COLLEGE if you cannot act like a young adult in pursuit of an education.

By defacing things you disagree with, in the name of the God in whom we trust, you don't deserve to be called American (if indeed you are), or a Christian or maybe a Jew. . We Americans welcomed you and your religious preference and your accent or maybe the way you dress. GET BORN AGAIN in love and in the American spirit! There's no room for trash in Christianity, in America, nor on this Campus!

You have another option. Step forward, face up to your act and erase this ignorance from your soul- your soul, the gift of God which you have defaced.

ONCE UPON A TIME

To the Blessed Sacrament Rosary Society Oct. 2007

I want to tell you a story. And a good tale often begins "Once Upon a Time..."
The name of my story: The Cinderella of Montreal- . Marie Marguerite d'Youville.
I begin the story: Once upon a time"!

Once upon a time in a small town called Varennes near Montreal Canada, a daughter was born to Cristophe Dufrost de Lajemmarais and Marie-Renée Gaultier de Varennes. The father, Christophe died young leaving his family of six in poverty.

Can you imagine the setting! Here is a poor, fatherless family. Out of it a daughter from among brother and sister siblings would one day be named saint! It reminds me of Cinderella- you all know that story- She would rise from her difficulties to become a princess and in my story another would rise to become saint. . Cinderella listened to the Good Fairy, Marguerite to the grace of God and love of Jesus.

Saint! Marguerite was proclaimed saint in 1990. Her life had resembled that of many people you may know, each having some life struggle. Do you know someone who lost a parent or children, someone in a difficult marriage, someone beset by in-law problems, someone who has experienced difficulty with a priest or other clergy, someone ridiculed because of her piety or goodness...???

Our Cinderella was a woman whose life was filled with each of these burdens, these obstacles. But... she overcame them and became a princess of the Church triumphant. That means she is a saint in heaven! (You know that we who are living are called the Church militant...)

But I jumped ahead of my story. There was a radio personality who used to say: Now here's the rest of the story.

So here is the rest of the story. It begins with the birth of Marguerite on October 15th 1701 and her baptism- the 16th! (I thought it was special, providential, that Paula asked me to do this presentation today on that

156

anniversary of my founder).

Because her father died when she was young, the male figure in her life was her grandfather. From him she learned to trust in God and God's Providence in all things. She went to school for 2 years. She left school to help her mother with the other children at home.

From her Ursuline teachers she learned to love the Cross of Christ and the Sacred Heart of Jesus. This opened her to what we call the French School of Spirituality- a contemplative spirit, and living the attitudes of Jesus.

This woman, Marguerite, married at 21, was widowed in 1730 at 29, was left with 2 sons aged 6 and 1. .And, pregnant at the time of her husband's death, totally without financial resources, she might have considered- in today's terms- going to window 7 at the Rath Bldg. looking for welfare!!!

Let me tell you about her marriage and her husband Francois d'Youville She married for love but her happiness was short lived. Her mother in-law was harsh to her and Francois became involved in illicit trading with the natives (liquor), stayed away from home much of the time and died of his own lifestyle of drink and infidelity. Not yet 30 Marguerite had buried 4 children. Now she was left with 2 sons, her husband's very bad reputation and considerable debts.

Anyway, this determined and independent young mother did not go to a window "7." About now you expect me to say she went to the ball and lost her slipper and a young prince found it and her and made her a princess...and she lived happily ever after...right? Wrong!

She did 2 things. (1) Opened a dry goods store to provide for her family. (2) Joined a Church group (Holy Family Society???) - much like you have done by joining the Rosary Society- to deepen her spiritual life and help those worse than herself. She joined with a few other women to serve the poor in Montreal.

How it is that we are called "Grey Nuns"? Marguerite and her associates were wearing grey dresses. The word for grey is "gris" But it also has another meaning- "tipsy", drunken. People who knew her and Francois' reputation mocked her, and her companions, as they would go to Mass calling them Les Sours Gris... the tipsy sisters. Her response was that "we will keep that name".

The first religious congregation was founded in Montreal with the name The Sisters of Charity of Montreal BUT called Grey Nuns...using the initials sgm- les sours gris. Interesting that the impact of the sisters was such that the citizens of Montreal turned the original slur into affection. They would say, "Go to the Grey Nuns, they never refuse to serve". Five more congregations were formed out of this one, each keeping the name and the commitment to serve any need. At her canonization, John Paul II named her Mother of Universal Charity.

The Sisters of Charity of Ottawa- the Grey Nuns of the Cross had spread into New York State opening schools and a college. It soon became necessary for an English speaking novitiate to continue the work they had begun. One hundred and fifty sisters responded and left to become an independent American branch. On Aug. 24, 1921, the Grey Nuns of the Sacred Heart came into being. We began on the West Side of Buffalo with Holy Angels grade school, Holy Angels High School and d'Youville College

Our ministry has responded to the signs and needs of the times. At the encouragement of Vatican II sisters realized that their gifts could serve a wide variety of needs. So today, our hands are open to the needy in many ways. In Buffalo, and Western NY alone, you find Grey Nuns serving the needy. Our ministry as a congregation stretches across the US from New York State to Kodiak Island Alaska.

But here in western New York....Names sound familiar?

Holy Angels Academy, d'Youville College, Erie Community College, Monroe Community College, St. Gregory the Great School, Renaissance House for teen alcoholics, Catholic Charities Social Work, Kenmore Mercy Hospital, Baker Victory Services, Columban Retreat Center, Kevin Guest House, Holy Cross Parish, Albion School System, Albion Correctional Facility, Christ the King Seminary, Private Clinical Social Work, Private Counselor...

We are about 30 sisters in this area. We are prompted to respond to

Marguerite's prayer to multiply our works of charity by devoting ourselves to such a wide variety of needs. Each is offering ministry and a witness to others so that all people can believe in love and justice and respond to the voice of those in need.

God calls each of us, regardless of being in religious or lay lifestyle, to respond to the needs of his people, our parishes have organizations to offer service opportunities. Religious Congregations have, Our GN congregation has, women and men who choose to be Associates and to carry on the charism of Marguerite d'Youville, indeed their baptismal call, in their response to the needy.

May God bless you, members of the Rosary Society, on your spiritual journey, for your service and the witness you are to God's people.

WHO'S AFRAID OF HARRY POTTER?

Some Christian groups have denounced Harry Potter using biblical mandates against wizardry and magic to support their stand. Most of the negative comments that I have heard are made without their having read the books or seen the movie

I think of all the wonderful fantasy I grew up with- the Grims' Tales, Cinderella, Snow White, Alice in Wonderland, The Wizard of Oz, The Hobbit, and ever so many fairy tales.... These stories were not devoid of witches, wizards and magic. But they were an enticement for me to read, to find happy hours in our local library. They challenged my young imagination to enter more than a world of fantasy; they encouraged me to want to tell my own tales, to allow my creativity to find expression in reading and in art.

Catholics are not afraid of Harry Potter. Our position rests on the value of positive fantasy (beats those violent video games). We live our faith without indulging in wizardry or magic or witchcraft. We can pray using one of God's gifts to us, our imaginations. In some forms of meditation we use our ability to fantasize, to imagine, in order to enter to enter the world of Jesus in any gospel story.

So, to all who are afraid of Harry Potter, then hang loose and read the book or see the movie. The overriding theme promoted through this piece of fantasy is love, "a love ... he received from his mother who sacrificed her life so Harry would live." Hmmm, where have I heard something like that before??

A WOMNAN'S CHRISTMAS PRAYER

Spirit
    of the Divine...
You come
    with no ceremony of arrival
    and Son us with your life.
Let us be
    the body'd mystery of your presence-
    woman'd, friend'd, responsible'd
    faith'd, office'd, Christ'd,
    compassion'd, apostl'd,
    youth'd, wise'd,
    listen'd, holy'd.
Spirit
    of the Divine...
    seeing the body
    "they" will wonder
    that infinity is here, now.
Spirit...
We are
    your pilgrims walking
    hand in hand...Divine'd. Amen

SANTA'S BAG OF JOY

Everyone
has his bag-
this thing
he must do.

Yahweh
had his love-
and love
brought forth all.

But all
turned away-
of love
it cried: Blood!

Jesus
son of love-
was born
bearing hope.

Everyone
has his bag-
this thing
he must do.

God-man
came with hope-
and hope
heartened all...

For all
one man spoke-
in hope
God's will be done!

Christ-Lord
exalted-
in death
kindling faith.

Everyone
has his bag-
this thing
he must do.
Spirit
stirring faith-
and faith
would save all.

Now all
sup as one-
ion faith
drink his cup.

Love-pact
sealed in wine-
new life
in this sign

Everyone
has his bag-
this thing
he must do.

\Joy-sign
that's our bag-
our thing
brought to all...

'fore all
we witness-
sign of
Christed man.

Our words
and our acts-
his life
must reveal.

Everyone
has his bag-
this thing
he must do.

Nicholas
saint of old-
loving
children all...

To all
good genius-
his deeds
done in Christ.

Saintly
vestige-
his "life"
dare we doubt?

EVERYONE
HAS HIS BAG-
WHO'ER
HE MAY BE-
THIS THING
HE MUST DO...

New Year
host of Joy-
gain'st doubt
lighting all...

That all
glean his grace-
see Joy
in everything.

Joy-light
flow'r of peace-
buds forth
in friends dear!